FLASHBACKS

A Vietnam Soldier's Story
50 Years Later

FLASHBACKS

A Vietnam Soldier's Story 50 Years Later

R. DEAN JERDE
AND TOM PISAPIA

LUMINARE PRESS

WWW.LUMINAREPRESS.COM

Printed in the United States of America

Cover Design by Melissa K. Thomas

Luminare Press
442 Charnelton St.
Eugene, OR 97401
www.luminarepress.com

LCCN: 2020913709
ISBN: 978-1-64388-419-6

DEDICATION

I would like to dedicate this book to my parents, Cliff and Carrie, for teaching me the values that sustained me throughout my life and gave me the courage to endure the war and these many years that followed.

I also dedicate this book to my GI buddies who did not make it back and to those who did but continue to fight their battles each day from within.

And most importantly, I dedicate this book to my Lord God who watched over me in all my times of need and answered my fervent prayers from the jungles of Vietnam. Thank you, Lord.

R. Dean Jerde

PREFACE

Ronald Dean Jerde spent over thirteen months in Vietnam from late 1967 to early 1969. He never spoke a word of those days until he had retired. It was not his choice to begin reminiscing about those experiences. His subconscious returned him to the jungles of Vietnam during his many sleepless nights in retirement. As these flashbacks became more frequent, Dean started to talk to his brother Paul and me, on occasion. Paul and I have been close friends for forty-five years and, although I knew Dean over that same period, we had not spent as much time together.

His random thoughts were disjointed at first, sometimes repetitive and difficult to follow. I was extremely uncomfortable even listening to some of his revelations at first, but was even more fearful of asking questions or any clarification. My psychology degree had at least taught me enough to know that I could easily do more harm than good by probing too much.

We began meeting two to three times per week for a year-and-a-half. During that time, Dean became more comfortable and his communications became more cohesive. We started sending each other emails regarding events. And I even got up the courage to ask questions and for clarifications.

As this communication increased, a format evolved. Dean would talk about a specific event and I would do the relevant research and commentary. Throughout the book, Dean's direct commentary is distinguished by "quotation marks."

During this process, I offered Dean anonymity as the revelations became more personal. He not only chose to use his real name but to coauthor the book.

It was my honor and privilege to have been present to record these memoirs. It is our hope and prayer that we can encourage other war veterans to come forward for help.

Tom Pisapia

CHAPTER 1

Why Now?

Why would I write a book about Vietnam now—over fifty years after leaving that sunny hamlet in Southeast Asia? There have been hundreds, if not thousands, of books and articles written on this war, both nonfiction and fiction, by more talented writers. Stories have already been told better by soldiers braver, who won more medals, served longer, saved more lives, and endured more hardships. Yet there is a valid reason for my telling of this story now. I must!

Like many GIs, I returned after my tour of duty in February 1969 and immediately immersed myself in everything to forget what I had experienced. I got married in 1971, had children in 1972 and 1975. I built my own house from scratch in 1980 and, of course, resumed my craft as a carpenter just as if nothing had changed.

I couldn't totally forget what I had experienced in Vietnam. There were many things that I saw or heard or thought about that immediately brought me back to the life in the rubber trees. But with all that I had to occupy my mind with a wife, work, and family, they became fewer, less severe, and more time passed between flashbacks.

I had worked nonstop for forty-three years, raised two sons, attended hundreds of kids' sporting and musical events, and been married to the same woman for over forty years.

I managed to bury most of my thoughts of that one year, one month, and ten days that I spent in Vietnam deep within my psyche and made sure that I never ever spoke one word of those events over the next fifty years—not to my wife, my children, my brothers, or even the closest of friends.

After all that I had been through during my military service, the welcome home was the last straw. Being greeted at every airport layover, not by a cheering and grateful public embrace for our brave service but by protesters calling us baby killers. Then, as we sought shelter and camaraderie at our local VFW so we could commiserate with our own kind, to be shunned by the veterans of World War II and Korea because "you didn't win your war." There was nothing else that I could do but bury my very thoughts from everyone and even myself for half a century.

During this period of denial, I didn't even use the local VA hospital for any medical services. Maybe it was still too close to the Vietnam memory, or maybe deep down I felt that there were veterans who needed the VA hospital more than I did—those warriors who were suffering more severely in both mind and body for a very long time.

Flash forward to 2008 and at age sixty-one, it was finally time to retire. A well-deserved rest from a busy and fruitful career awaited me. It was time to enjoy life with my wife and do those things that the two of us had postponed doing those many years, deferring our own needs and wants to provide for those of the children.

However, as soon as my body and mind realized that I was not on vacation and didn't have the pressure and distraction of work on that next Monday morning, a change took place. No longer fully occupied with thoughts of work and family demands, my mind had time to wander.

Consciously, I had not noticed any change except that I now had time to do all those postponed projects around the house. But subconsciously, my mind was now free to drift back in time and explore long-ignored experiences, especially during the nighttime previously reserved for sleep. Soon my mind began dredging up those thoughts from fifty years ago in the rubber trees in the jungles of Vietnam. Flashbacks to the life and, more powerfully, the deaths in war found a renewed platform in my psyche.

At first, it seemed like an isolated incident, a bad dream that startled me from a sound sleep and found me sweating heavily in my own bed. But, the frequency and intensity of these flashbacks increased as was repeatedly confirmed by my wife—a wife who, still, after all these years of marriage, knew nothing about the most traumatic period of her husband's life. I had kept these secrets so closely guarded from everyone but now they were manifesting themselves beyond my control. I was no longer able to repress and control these thoughts. They had taken on a life of their own during my nights and soon my waking hours as well.

Ironically, an affliction also linked to the war became the catalyst that forced me to engage with my local VA hospital. After experiencing some chronic hearing difficulty since the constant pounding of the big guns at Fire Support Base (FSB) Buttons in Vietnam, now my hearing had become even worse. It seems the incessant H&I (Harassment & Interdiction) fire to keep the Viet Cong or North Vietnamese Army (NVA) troops at bay had finally taken its toll.

This controversial tactic required the firing of a few rounds from the heavy guns at random intervals throughout the night and sometimes during the day as well. The fire was meant to deny the enemy freedom of movement and to destroy enemy morale. It is estimated that the Army used nearly half of all its ammunition during 1966 and 1967 on H&I fire.

My local doctor confirmed tinnitus, a ringing or buzzing noise in one or both ears that may be constant or come and go, often associated with hearing loss.

My doctor recommended hearing aids, but the cost was prohibitive. He commented that since I had been in the military, I should contact the VA hospital and perhaps it could be of assistance.

After the routine information was gathered by the VA staff and doctors, they confirmed the tinnitus diagnosis but also required that I meet with the VA psych doctor. Thus, the process of discussing those fifty-year-old memories began to reveal themselves, opening long overdue conversations about Vietnam, not only with my doctor but just as importantly with my wife, sons, and brother.

Tom Pisapia

Since this healing is still a work in progress as I write this memoir, I can't tell you how the story ends. But I know that I am moving in the right direction and am optimistic that I am finally on the right path.

Tens of thousands of Vietnam veterans are waking up to this new reality about their war experience. Feelings and thoughts, both conscious and unconscious, now flood their minds as they make the difficult transition into retirement. This period is very challenging for many retirees under normal circumstances, but the Vietnam veterans had no idea that they would now, fifty years later, have to confront, once again, the trauma of war.

Any logical person would realize that this delayed post-traumatic stress disorder, or PTSD syndrome, is not limited to Vietnam War-era veterans. All those warriors who have served in our armed conflicts around the globe since Vietnam and continuing today would certainly seem susceptible to this retirement-triggered experience as well. Considering veterans who fought in Iraq and

Afghanistan and develop PTSD but are still quite young, sadly they may have a similar retirement experience awaiting them.

If by writing these memoirs, I can help just one other veteran open up about his or her experience in Vietnam and help them to find closure, as I hope that I will myself, then I will have accomplished my final mission.

PTSD

Like most mental illnesses, PTSD is not strictly curable. This condition is caused by trauma and causes serious symptoms that make normal functioning challenging or impossible. Treatment with special types of therapy and sometimes medication can make a big difference, but it is not a cure.

PTSD is diagnosed after a person experiences symptoms for at least one month following a traumatic event. However, symptoms may not appear until several months or even years later. The disorder is characterized by three main types of symptoms:

- re-experiencing the trauma through intrusive distressing recollections of the event, flashbacks, and nightmares

- emotional numbness and avoidance of places, people, and activities that are reminders of the trauma

- increased arousal such as difficulty sleeping and concentrating, feeling jumpy, and being easily irritated and angered

PTSD can also result from exposure to actual or threatened death, serious injury, or sexual violation:

- directly experiencing the traumatic events

- witnessing, in person, the traumatic events

- learning that the traumatic events occurred to a close family member or close friend; cases of actual or threatened death must have been violent or accidental

- experiencing repeated or extreme exposure to aversive details of the traumatic events (Examples are first responders collecting human remains; police officers repeatedly exposed to details of child abuse). Note: This does not apply to exposure through electronic media, television, movies, or pictures unless exposure is work-related.

PTSD is characterized by the presence of one or more of the following:

- spontaneous or cued recurrent, involuntary, and intrusive distressing memories of the traumatic events

- recurrent distressing dreams in which the content or affect (i.e., feeling) of the dream is related to the events

- flashbacks or other dissociative reactions in which the individual feels or acts as if the traumatic events are recurring

Tom Pisapia

- intense or prolonged psychological distress at exposure to internal or external cues that symbolize or resemble an aspect of the traumatic events

- physiological reactions to reminders of the traumatic events

Screen yourself or a family member for PTSD.
Persistent avoidance of distressing memories, thoughts, or feelings about or closely associated with the traumatic events or of external reminders (i.e., people, places, conversations, activities, objects, situations)
Two or more of the following:

- inability to remember an important aspect of the traumatic events (not due to head injury, alcohol, or drugs)

- persistent and exaggerated negative beliefs or expectations about oneself, others, or the world (e.g., "I am bad," "No one can be trusted," "The world is completely dangerous")

- persistent, distorted blame of self or others about the cause or consequences of the traumatic events

- persistent fear, horror, anger, guilt, or shame

- markedly diminished interest or participation in significant activities

- feelings of detachment or estrangement from others

- persistent inability to experience positive emotions

Two or more of the following marked changes in arousal and reactivity:

- irritable or aggressive behavior

- reckless or self-destructive behavior

- hypervigilance

- exaggerated startle response

- problems with concentration

Tom Pisapia

- difficulty falling or staying asleep or restless sleep

Also, clinically significant distress or impairment in social, occupational, or other important areas of functioning not attributed to the direct physiological effects of medication, drugs, or alcohol or another medical condition, such as traumatic brain injury.

Check out the mobile app "PTSD Coach," from the US Department of Veterans Affairs, https://www.ptsd.va.gov/appvid/mobile/ptsdcoach_app.asp. The PTSD Coach has now been downloaded over 500,000 times in 115 countries around the world.

The PTSD Coach app can help you learn about and manage symptoms that often occur after trauma. Features include:

- reliable information on PTSD and treatments that work

- tools for screening and tracking your symptoms

- convenient, easy-to-use tools to help you handle stress symptoms

- direct links to support and help

- always with you when you need it

Mayo Clinic adds:

PTSD symptoms can vary in intensity over time. You may have more PTSD symptoms when you are stressed in general, or when you come across reminders of what you went through. For example, you may hear a car backfire and relive combat experiences. Or you may see a report on the news about a sexual assault and feel overcome by memories of your own assault.

The most common events leading to the development of PTSD include:

- combat exposure

- childhood physical abuse

- sexual violence

Tom Pisapia

- physical assault

- being threatened with a weapon

- an accident

For more information, visit these websites:

https://www.ptsd.va.gov/index.asp

https://adaa.org/understanding-anxiety/
posttraumatic-stress-disorder-ptsd/symp-
toms

https://www.mayoclinic.org/diseases-condi-
tions/post-traumatic-stress-disorder/diagno-
sis-treatment/drc-2035597

CHAPTER 2

The Journey Begins

Ronald Dean Jerde grew up in DeKalb, a small rural town in Illinois, about sixty miles west of Chicago but a world away. Then, as well as today, DeKalb was known for corn and the flying ear of corn symbol that was proudly displayed in the fields in every direction surrounding the town. Today about 155,000 acres in DeKalb County alone are still devoted to growing their favorite crop.

Dean was the second youngest of seven children, and he and his siblings were raised in a strict and deeply religious family by his parents, Carrie and Cliff. His father, along with his entire family, maintained close ties to their fundamentalist Lutheran church where his father even served as an assistant pastor on occasion.

As little kids, the Jerde children were encouraged by their mother to play outdoors. Often, the locked screen door served as a subtle notice to do just that. Dean, along with his brothers and sisters, were very creative at finding various ways to entertain themselves, especially Dean.

One summer day, when Dean was three years old and his sister Carmen was four, they were playing in their backyard near the garage. An alley ran from the garage along the side of their house to Prospect Street.

Their family owned a serviceable black-and-white, two-toned 1952 Chevy. It was not unusual for cars of that era to be equipped with a push-button starter on the dashboard instead of an ignition key. After the driver depressed the clutch, the button was pushed to start the car.

However, the three-year-old Dean discovered that if he pressed the starter button, the car would lunge forward until he released it. Certainly, neither he nor his sister ever thought of depressing the clutch, even if they knew what it was for, their legs were far too short to reach it!

So, one day Dean decided to take his sister for a car ride down the alley and on to Prospect Street by pressing the starter button repeatedly. Each time they pressed it, the car would lunge forward a few feet until they finally reached Prospect Street. There the two kids sat, talking and laughing and carrying on, while positioned on the huge bench seat of the Chevy.

Soon, their mother happened to peer out through the locked screen door and noticed that she could not see the kids nor the family car! Quickly, their joy ride was over, and although their mother was mad, she was more relieved that the kids weren't hurt.

The Grand Theft Auto Duo
and the '52 Chevy

As Dean grew into his teens, his curiosity and creativity continued to grow as well. He enjoyed using his hands along with his imagination to build things and solve problems, but sometimes his ingenuity created some problems too. Whether he was making home-made stilts out of scraps of wood or rigging lights for night basketball games or building a pole vault pit so he could practice at home, his creativity shone through.

But freezing the driveway for a hockey rink put him on the wrong side of his dad and his Uncle Olie, who lived next door. With the gravel driveway now turned to ice, they could no longer get their cars up the incline and into their garages.

These early projects served Dean well as he became a professional carpenter, builder, and problem-solver at the highest level of construction.

As Dean worked his way through high school, like all kids his age, he longed to graduate and spread his wings. Shedding strict rules and the blustery weather in northern

Illinois supplied more than enough motivation to want a change of location and all the freedom that it would provide.

In the fall of 1966, Dean entered Miami-Dade College in Miami, Florida, many states and many miles away from the cold weather and restrictions that had been part of his daily life in the Midwest. However, Miami-Dade was not just about the weather and the distance. The college also boasted a flight training curriculum that could prepare Dean for a career in commercial aviation which, at the time, was his goal.

Unfortunately, his college experience was short-lived, and, after one semester, he was forced to return to the frigid Midwest at the request of his local draft board. The next step became inevitable. Every young man who did not have a student deferment by passing thirty semester hours of college-credit courses per year immediately became draft fodder to fill the insatiable appetite for soldiers to serve in the Vietnam War.

By the time Dean would return from Vietnam, his interest in being a pilot would wane. His frequent flying in helicopters through the jungles would taint his love of aviation... just one of the many things that the war would change for Dean and the GIs who served with him.

However, Dean was chosen to drive another vehicle that required him to draw on his early experience using a starter button. Unfortunately, he had no additional training or desire to navigate a jeep in Vietnam outfitted with a 120-million candlepower searchlight that turned night into day, as he illuminated the way for a deuce and a half truck with Quad 50 machine guns, so that they could find and destroy their targets in the jungles of Vietnam.

Tom Pisapia

Jeep with Mounted Searchlight

CHAPTER 3

Mid-July 1967

We have all heard stories about the rigors of basic training or boot camp, but we should take a closer look at just what the daily routine in this eight-week challenge involved. As soon as revelry sounded, we assembled for some daily calisthenics including push-ups, sit-ups, squats, and jumping jacks followed by a brisk mile-and-a-half run.

At breakfast, we would stand in the food line, take our food, find a seat, and eat quickly because there were so many troops right behind us waiting to eat. Lunch was the same, with several companies of hungry men fed in that same hour.

Each day was a repeat of the previous

one. We would attend classes on personal hygiene and, more importantly, on cleaning our weapons plus the dos and don'ts of being a soldier. Keeping our boots polished was an endless job. They taught us how to spit-shine them plus what it took to clean and organize our footlockers to pass our numerous inspections which, of course, included being able to bounce a quarter off our bunk blanket.

We ran everywhere! We ran to calisthenics, we ran to breakfast, to the rifle range to train with our M-14s, and to the grenade range to train with live grenades. The Army planned everything for us and we were constantly reminded that we were Army property and don't forget it! But, by the time we graduated, we were in the best shape of our lives.

The lack of sleep and continuous physical challenges in boot camp weighed heavily on all the recruits or "grunts" as we were better known. Few humorous stories came out of basic training and maybe that's why we just laughed a little harder at them because it was so grueling, physically and mentally, and seemed to never stop. One particular GI in our barracks had a rather unusual reaction every time inspection was called, and he stood at attention in front of his bunk. His name was Charlie Brown and he always got an erection when he stood at attention.

Fortunately, this peculiar anomaly was not widespread and perhaps it could just have been an unusual reaction to stress. But, one day during a routine inspection, as the officer walked up and down, stopping to scrutinize each soldier's bunk and uniform and always finding something wrong with each man, he glanced down and saw this young soldier standing at attention with an erection. Without hesitation, the officer blurted out, "You must be Charlie Brown!"

CHAPTER 4

Mid-September 1967

As soon as Dean completed his grueling eight weeks of basic training or boot camp, he was immediately sent to AIT (Advanced Individual Training) at Fort Huachuca in Cochise County, in southeast Arizona, about fifteen miles north of the border with Mexico and at the northern end of the Huachuca Mountains, next to the town of Sierra Vista.

Fort Huachuca is a US Army installation and also the headquarters of Army Military Auxiliary Radio System (MARS). Since Dean's MOS (military occupational specialty) had been designated as radio and teletype, he certainly was being sent to the right place to perfect his craft.

By no coincidence, Fort Huachuca also housed the school for linemen. There they would train the GIs that would physically string the wire so that communication was possible. As one might imagine, these men also had to practice pole climbing, wearing spiked boots, and securing belts around the poles to control their climbing and controlled descent.

The practice was so intense and frequent that the poles soon became worn from all the use. They became so splintered that the men would lose their footing and slide until they could gain control. This unexpected descent often left them with splinters in their calves—some six inches in length that had to be cut out before they could return to training, where the same fate awaited them again and again during their thirteen weeks of AIT training.

The pressure of studying Morse code, being able to hear and transcribe so many infinitesimal dots and dashes and convert-ing them into error-free communications, posed a daunting challenge. Speed was also essential, and Dean was required to process at least sixty-five words per minute to pass the proficiency standard. He knew that his performance needed to be flawless because lives would depend on it.

Finally, after four weeks of this constant drudgery, Dean got a break—a two-day pass!

Now, where could four young GIs enjoy a furlough in this remote corner of Arizona? Of course, Nogales, Mexico, just across the border where a constant fiesta raged and bullfights to boot!

In the 1950s and '60s, Arizona tourists and Hollywood stars alike filled the stands in the old Plaza de Toros in Nogales to see some of the world's most famous bullfighters perform just south of the border. It was said that up to four thousand people could be heard many blocks away yelling "Ole!" at the same time.

Dean and his buddies had no trouble joining in the fiesta atmosphere as soon as they bought some botas and an ample supply of Boone's Farm wine to fill their wine skins to the brim. As was the custom and a good idea, they also bought plastic seat cushions for the arena, not as much for their comfort but to keep a barrier between them and the filth of the arena.

They were still just a bunch of twenty-year-old kids wearing "civies" that day and blending in with the other tourists. Except for their closely cropped haircuts, they could have passed for college kids on spring break.

Had they been the ones who were still in school rather than AIT in the Army, they might have been going to Fort Lauderdale instead of Fort Huachuca. They were the same age but doing incredibly different things and that gap between the two groups would only grow. Dean's group would soon mature way too abruptly and never have the chance to have that carefree college experience that students so easily took for granted.

As they entered the arena with their botas and cushions in hand, they became one with the throng of spectators, as they found some seats. They felt the same excitement they would have expected at an American football game between their favorite team and a hated rival. The difference in this arena that it was hosting a contest between a man and an animal, with death and perhaps grave injury a certitude.

It is impossible to relate that day in Nogales with our GIs without reflecting on a day in Pamplona in *The Sun Also Rises*....

"Romero was...getting so close that the bull could see him plainly, offering the body, offering it again a little closer, the bull watching dully, then so close that the bull thought he had him, offering again and finally drawing the charge and then, just before the horns came, giving the bull the red cloth to follow with that little, almost imperceptible, jerk...."

The young matador Romero in this Ernest Hemingway classic was the same age as Dean and his pals. He had practiced his craft for most of his young life. He chose to risk his life in the ring with an angry bull over and over, for more than the money but for the praise and fame that came with bullfighting.

Our young GIs were soon to be put to much more lethal tests in the jungles of Vietnam with a cunning and ruthless enemy who knew the terrain much better and whose only goal was to kill GIs whom they had never even met. Our GIs engaged this enemy not for praise or fame and certainly not for money but simply for the love of their country.

The Nogales sun was a little lower in the sky as the last bull collapsed to his knees, succumbing to the matador's sword plunged to the hilt between his shoulders. They yelled "Ole!" in unison with the frenzied crowd and hurled their no-longer-needed seat cushions into the arena.

Then, as they squirted the last ounces of cheap wine into their mouths, they finished their celebration and headed back across the border to Fort Huachuca. Tomorrow their training would resume right where it left off, without missing a beat. But they would take a few memories of their time away from the base with them and occasionally reflect on them during less-than-pleasant moments in Southeast Asia.

For the next thirteen weeks, Dean's training would continue until he became proficient. He was comfortable and confident in his ability to perform all the radio and teletype duties. They had to become second nature since he knew that he would be performing them under combat conditions. Unfortunately, there was no way to practice that added challenge until faced with the real thing.

As AIT ended, Dean received a well-deserved two-week leave and was able to return to DeKalb to visit family and friends, hopefully not for the last time. His next stop would be Oakland, California, followed by Hawaii for a three-hour layover and a stop in Guam, then on to Tan Son Nhut Air Base, Vietnam. It would be Christmas 1967 when he would first set foot on Vietnam soil.

Dean's enlistment photo

Tom Pisapia

CHAPTER 5

Late December 1967

As on any long air flight—and this 16-hour one from Guam was no exception—Dean alternated between getting up and stretching his legs and taking a few catnaps, waking up from each with a start and briefly forgetting where he was. After all, this was just a normal commercial flight on a standard Boeing 707 except for the presence of 175 freshly minted soldiers wearing Army-issue fatigues and each carrying an identical duffel bag with all their worldly personal effects.

As he was about to land at Tan Son Nhut Air Base in Vietnam, the pilot came on the intercom and began to speak in that matter-of-fact official pilot voice, sounding annoyingly cool and calm. All were expecting the usual admonitions about seat-belt-fastening, pushing the tray tables upright, and extinguishing all smoking materials in the handy ashtray in the armrest.

Instead, it caught all the passengers by surprise as they heard, in a somewhat agitated, non-pilot-like voice, "When we land, head for the bunkers!" The GI next to Dean piped up with justified concern in a loud voice. "Where are the bunkers?" One of the other soldiers quickly put him at ease by yelling, "You'll find out!" So, the journey began.

The doughnut and cup of coffee at the Eagles Club in DeKalb, Illinois, that he enjoyed before boarding a train to begin this odyssey on July 12, 1967, seemed like years ago but would be remembered later since a fresh doughnut and cup of hot coffee would become scarce commodities for many months to come.

———————

Tan Son Nhut Air Base was located near the city of Saigon in southern Vietnam. The

United States used it as a major base during the Vietnam War, stationing Army, Air Force, Navy, and Marine units there. Following the fall of Saigon, it was taken over as a Vietnam People's Air Force (VPAF) facility and remains in use today.

The two days that Dean spent at Tan Son Nhut would seem like a vacation getaway compared to his next destination. After getting outfitted at the base with jungle fatigues, jungle boots and an M-16, he boarded a UH-1 helicopter better known to all as a Huey, with three other GI passengers. The Huey already was occupied by its crew consisting of a pilot, co-pilot, and two door gunners, one on each side of the Huey with the doors wide open. The gunners each embraced a .50-caliber machine gun and made it obvious that their job was to keep the Huey and its occupants safe from ground fire from the hidden enemy below.

Perhaps what comes next is best said by Dean in his own words:

"Then we were put on a helicopter to go to Fire Base Buttons by Song Be. The ride was quite an experience, especially when you hear the roar of the big engines and the propellers batting in the wind. We were strapped in with a seat belt and that was it. So, off we go.

"The pilot would make his turns and when you looked out all you could see was the ground. It was a weird feeling. All you would see is jungle, rice paddies, and thousands of ponds made from all the shelling and bombs dropped. I'll never forget the sound of the blades with the woop, woop sound. Sitting next to me was a door gunner. I looked at him and he looked at me and gave me a thumbs up. At that moment I thought to myself, 'What have they got me into here?' Frightening! So we landed at the fire base with the dust from the chopper blowing that dusty red clay all over. The first thing through my mind was, 'What happens next?' But as the saying goes, 'You'll find out.' There was always some troop ready to show you the next step."

Door gunner's .50-caliber—UH-1 Huey

The helicopter trip lasted only about an hour but seemed like an eternity and, by all measures, it was. Tan Son Nhut Air Base was a relatively safe and secure place when compared to the innocently named destination of Fire Base Buttons, officially called Song Be FSB Buttons.

CHAPTER 6

Song Be FSB Buttons

Late December 1967

"As the chopper approached the landing zone, I looked down to see a compound that stuck out of the jungle. It was the color of red clay. All the foliage was dead due to the spraying of Agent Orange. There was a berm around the base with several rolls of concertina wire surrounding it, bunkers, an airstrip, a helicopter pad, and big guns on tracks—175, 8-inch and 105. I wondered to myself, 'Why am I here?'"

Dean at the perimeter of Song Be
FSB Buttons.

Dean was not delivered to a randomly constructed encampment, rather this firebase configuration was repeated throughout Vietnam as the military created these forward zones to provide safety for their advancing troops. This particular firebase warrants additional commentary.

Fire Support Base Buttons, formerly called LZ Buttons, was once one of the largest bases in the area of northeastern III Corps. Over the years, it was home to Army units together with all kinds of support and flying units. Being located so close to the Cambodian border meant that Buttons blocked the way for PAVN (People's Army of Vietnam) troops from infiltrating across the border.

The camp was also used as a staging ground during the Cambodian Incursion. Thanks to its proximity to Cambodia, choppers would lift off and be able to support the troops in Cambodia within minutes. Traffic went west toward the Fishhook region as well as north toward Snuol, Cambodia. Most of these larger camps would also host a Special Forces camp and Buttons was no exception.

Fire Support Base Buttons was the most northern of the large bases. The Song Be River runs all the way through the area. Its bridges were highly contested and especially the Song Be Bridge south of Phuoc Binh, which had a permanent guard unit. Viet Cong and NVA units would also use the river as an infiltration route, making it a hot spot. This was a very active area during the war.

In general, a fire support base was a large military camp enclosed and surrounded by two or three strands of concertina wire. Many FSBs were designed and constructed to accommodate a combat brigade head-quarters, an infantry battalion headquarters, an infantry company, artillery batteries, a cavalry troop, landing pads, and revetments for helicopters, vehicle and helicopter refu-eling points, dug-in and sandbagged fixed fighting positions around the perimeter, and dug-in and sandbagged bunkers for living areas with sandbagged overhead cover. Most of the larger FSBs were constructed to be a permanent military site.

On Google Earth, the general center loca-tion of FSB Buttons in 1969 is shown at lati-tude 106° 57′ 40.00″ E and longitude 11° 49′ 29.00″ N.

Song Be & Phuoc Long

Nui Ba Ra

Road 310/741

C123/C130 Airstrip
Song Be Airport

FSB Buttons

Road 311/759

Phuoc Binh

Road LTL1A

CALTEX

Google earth

Tom Pisapia

This airstrip, now indicated as the Song Be Airport, quite visible and prominent on Google Earth, was large enough and long enough to accommodate the US Air Force and US Army cargo workhorses: the twin-engine C-123 Provider, the twin-engine C-7 Caribou, and the four-engine C-130 Hercules.

The towns of Phuoc Long and Song Be were several kilometers east of Buttons. The town of Phuoc Binh was between one and two kilometers west.

In 1969, the east-west road between Phuoc Long and Phuoc Binh was Road 310. In Phuoc Binh, the east-west Road 310 and the north-south Road 311 formed a junction with Highway LTL1A. The junctions of Road 310 and LTL1A and Road 311 and LTL1A were so close together it seemed then, in 1969, that 310 and 311 intersected.

Road 310 ran between FSB Buttons and the airstrip (the Song Be Airport). Road 310 was outside the third strand of wire and paralleled the southern perimeter of Buttons. The airstrip was near the northeastern foot of Nui

Ba Ra. From the airstrip south to the base of the mountain was dense woods and jungle.

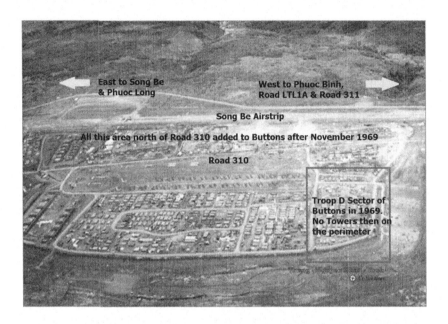

FSB Buttons, early 1970, aerial
photo by Ken Filmore

Nui Ba Ra, a volcano a million years old, is a small but predominant mountain rising up from relatively flat ground to a height of about 760 meters (about 2,300 feet) at its tallest peak. Nui Ba Ra was about one kilometer south and a little east of FSB Buttons and west of the towns of Phuoc Long and Song Be.

Tom Pisapia

Airstrip at FSB Buttons

Cargo helicopters at FSB Buttons

Beginning in late June through October 1969, Troop D from FSB Buttons conducted dismounted operations in the jungle and rubber plantations and mounted cavalry reconnaissance, scouting, screening, patrolling, and security missions along the vast and intricate network of trails, roads, highways, and other lines of communication throughout Phuoc Long Province. At night, Troop D occupied defensive positions on the western and northern sectors of the large, expansive perimeter of Buttons. Occasionally, Delta Troop would conduct squad or platoon-sized night ambushes outside Buttons.

Buttons was the headquarters base of the 5th Battalion, 7th Cavalry, of a howitzer battery consisting of six towed 105mm cannons and of Delta Troop.

Bunkers and sandbags at FSB Buttons

This artillery battery provided fire support for the 5th Battalion Infantry companies, the Scout Platoons, and for Delta Troop. "Garry Owen" was the title of the 5th Battalion, 7th Cavalry crest and the Irish tune George Armstrong Custer chose as the 7th Cavalry regimental song in 1867.

In late October 1969, Second Brigade Headquarters moved to Buttons from the 1st Cavalry Division Base Camp near Phuoc Vinh. Plans were in the works to double the size and capacity of Buttons, as evidenced by the relocation of the brigade headquarters and Tactical Operations Center (TOC).

Although Dean's MOS and lengthy training at Fort Huachuca was for radio and teletype, he was assigned to searchlight duty as soon as he arrived at Firebase Buttons. The searchlight operator on duty was a short-timer and soon would be heading home. Somehow, using perfect Army logic, that would make Dean the obvious replacement and to hell with his MOS!

The extensive training involved spending a couple of days with the GI he was about to replace. Of course, Dean had never even seen a huge searchlight mounted on a jeep before and was totally unaware of the piece of wartime history that was about to become his most dangerous full-time job. Dean was assigned to I BTRY (Battery) 29th Field Artillery—Search Light Division—Attached to the 101st Airborne, 1st Cavalry Division.

If you can imagine searchlights at war, you might picture troops scanning for enemy planes in Europe during World War II. But for the US Army, the Vietnam War was the last chance for its increasingly obsolete, high-powered lamps to shine.

Between 1965 and 1967, the Army deployed four searchlight batteries to South Vietnam. Technically artillery units, these soldiers spent most of their time keeping watch over friendly base camps, freeing up the infantry for other missions.

Army Brig. Gen. John Boles Jr., the director of the Pentagon's Joint Research and Test Activity, explained this in the introduction to a 1965 report on the potential utility of the lights. "As is generally known, one of the principal differences between counterinsurgency and conventional wars is that the majority of insurgent operations are conducted under the cover of darkness," he stated. "Therefore, illumination of the battle area has become vital."

Despite soldiering on throughout the conflict, the searchlights eventually fell victim to ever-improving night-vision gear.

By the time Battery B, 29th Artillery arrived at Qui Nhon in 1965, the searchlight was already showing its age as a weapon of war. American anti-aircraft gunners had already given up the lamps in favor of far more powerful radars.

Army artillerists were no strangers to the radar game either. The ground combat branch shipped AN/MPQ-4 units to Southeast Asia to look for enemy mortars and larger AN/TPS-25s to scan the battlefield in general.

Compared with these sleek-looking dishes and radomes, the 30-inch carbon arc lamps looked positively...archaic. An early nineteenth-century technology predating the incandescent light bulbs most people are familiar with, a carbon arc design produces an intense light by shooting a bolt of electricity between two electrodes.

A year before the first searchlight soldiers arrived in Vietnam, Army leaders had even recommended shutting down the last two active searchlight platoons. Instead, the ground combat branch decided that the World War II-era equipment had distinct advantages for fighting guerrillas and increased the size of the light units fivefold.

Most importantly, the gear was easy and cheap to use compared to the alternatives. Bad weather, fires, smoke and other environmental hazards could hamper planes flying in to drop illumination flares.

Soldiers could also point the beam of light exactly where it would be most useful. Focused to its brightest setting, the lamp could put out 400 million candlepower—far brighter than direct sunlight at noon—onto a target nearly ten thousand yards away. To a lesser degree, troops could brighten up the darkness across a broader area by bouncing the light off low-lying clouds or just shining it into the night sky.

But tests with the South Vietnamese Army showed that the system was far from perfect. Rain, fog, and physical obstructions limited the light. Hardly ideal for discreet operations on the move, the arc lamps needed a large and noisy gasoline-powered generator to keep running. And no matter where they were, the big, bright lights offered a huge target for enemy troops.

Nevertheless, American commanders concluded that the searchlight had a place in the war, particularly around outposts, bridges, and other facilities.

However, the fighting wasn't static. Viet Cong guerrillas would often distract attention to one side of a base before throwing their real weight from the other direction.

Combat engineers—commonly referred to as sappers—might try to breach defenses at various locations at once. The Army quickly realized that the heavy lamps were a pain to move into position during these complex attacks.

So, two years after deploying to Vietnam, Battery B traded in its 30-inch units for twice as many smaller 23-inch xenon searchlights. Similar to traditional arc lamps, these types shoot electricity between electrodes in a chamber full of ionized xenon gas.

In addition to being simpler and more efficient, the new AN/MSS-3 lights were small enough to fit on a standard M-151 jeep—and were able to put out beams in the visible or infrared spectrum. With special binoculars or telescopes, troops could see enemies without giving away their positions.

The lighter lamps only put out 120 million candlepower. The ability to quickly change positions during a fight easily offset any issue arising from the dimmer light.

When Battery B's sister units—Batteries G, H, and I, 29th Artillery—deployed to Vietnam, their soldiers already had the new lamps in hand.

In many cases, Army commanders paired the new trucks with anti-aircraft weapons to protect fire bases. With no threat of enemy air attacks, the ground combat branch turned its 40-millimeter M-42 tracked anti-aircraft vehicles of quadruple .50-caliber M-55 machine gun turrets on enemy guerrillas.

The Viet Cong took notice of the combination. In one 1968 report, the commander of 4th Battalion, 60th Artillery—one anti-aircraft unit with the searchlight teams attached to it—noted: "The employment of automatic weapons and searchlights has proven extremely effective not only in open engagement of the enemy but also a deterrent against enemy attacks."

At various sites, the jeeps conducted their own brand of the Army's "harassment and interdiction" missions. Usually performed by firing artillery shells at random into predetermined areas, the searchlight teams would instead shine their beams into those locations or nearby villages.

These so-called H & I strikes were supposed to keep insurgents on their toes, but often killed innocent civilians or wildlife instead. While nonlethal, the bright lights shining into people's homes in the middle of the night probably did not win any hearts and minds.

And despite their new mobile nature, the lights were still prime targets. "To fully exploit the capabilities of the jeep-mounted searchlight, it is necessary to move the light to several alternate positions each night," reported officers from 1st Battalion, 44th Artillery, in 1967.

Not that this necessarily mattered. The AN/MSS-3's infrared feature was already pointing toward a new future.

Early "Starlight Scopes" and other night vision gear were not particularly effective at long distances or in especially poor light. But engineers were steadily improving passive systems—those able to amplify existing light rather than needing an invisible light source like an infrared lamp.

In 1969, the Army shipped nine new AN/TVS-3 searchlights to South Vietnam. Three years earlier, the ground combat branch had started working on these 30-inch xenon units as a similarly powerful replacement for the older carbon arc designs.

While the new units were successful, the writing was on the wall. "The 30-inch xenon searchlight (would) be deployed ... on a mission-justified basis," the Army Concept Team in Vietnam evaluators wrote in their final report.

With Vietnamization in full swing and American and other friendly troops starting to pull out of the country, there just wasn't any point in developing more lamps of any kind. As of 1972, the last of the Army's searchlight units had packed up and left Southeast Asia.

Jeep with mounted searchlight

Although searchlights have had a long history in war, Dean's relationship with his own

Tom Pisapia

equipment was a rather brief but intense courtship. His searchlight was mounted on a jeep that he drove himself, following a deuce and a half with Quad .50-caliber machine guns and illuminating their way with infrared light in the jungle darkness, all using infrared binoculars until they spotted the enemy and it was time to engage them. At that moment, down went the binoculars and Dean lit up the jungle, turning night into day with 120 million candlepower and exposing himself to the enemy as well as making him their first target.

A stark reminder of combat, this jeep, with mounted searchlight, was from the 2nd Platoon of H Battery (SLT), 29th FA, and shows the damage resulting from the combat action that cost the life of SP4 Raymond Lee Jarvi and wounded three others on November 9, 1967.

Fortunately for Dean, as soon as the Quad 50s started firing, the enemy had other things on its mind as they dug down to dodge the quad's deadly fury.

The Quad 50 (M2, aka "Ma Duce") was mounted and operated in one frame. It was

Tom Pisapia

originally used during WWII as an aircraft weapon and nicknamed the "meat chopper" and "Krautmower" for its high rate of fire. The weapon consisting of four of the "HB," or "heavy barrel" .50 caliber M2 Browning machine guns, mounted in pairs on each side of an open, electrically powered turret.

The bullet is a half-inch round and about two inches long. The casing is three-quarters inch round and four inches long, producing a very powerful round.

There was a gun crew assigned to each deuce and a half consisted of a driver, gunner, and an ammo man on each side of the quad. The effective range was about a mile and it was capable of delivering well over one thousand rounds per minute, although the barrels would get red hot and start to warp if this rate was maintained for long periods.

In the .50-caliber chain link ammo, every fifth round is a tracer. The tracer rounds helped the gunner see what he was hitting and adjust his aim during night fire. Historically, tracers were used at the end on an ammo box to alert the ammo guys that they needed to reload. But the problem was that the enemy picked up on this practice too quickly and knew when the guns were running out of ammo.

When the quads opened fire, they would snap the rubber trees like match sticks. Even their six-to-eight-inch girth could not withstand the .50-caliber onslaught. The jungle was quickly transformed into a surreal landscape of uneven stubble, exposing the remains of an enemy that was too slow to outrun the carnage.

Deuce and a half with Quad
.50-caliber machine gun

Tom Pisapia

CHAPTER 7

Rats and Shit

Rats

"After being out spending nights in the jungle and rubber trees, we would go back to the fire base for supplies and to try and get some sleep, which was usually just catnaps. We would go into the underground bunkers, which consisted of a cot and a mosquito net, dirt floor, and a bowl, and a little mirror to wash the red clay off your face that had filtered through the sandbags and planking all night from the big guns firing H&I. The rats would run from one end of the bunker to the other, squeaking, and then run to the opposite end.

"One night while trying to sleep, I had my mosquito net around me on the cot. When I awoke, I could feel something crawling up the side of my leg. I laid there petrified. I could feel something now crawling up my side close to my neck. I couldn't take it anymore and I let out a yell and flew out of my cot to a standing position in the dark facing my cot. Everyone in the bunker was awake now and wanted to know what was going on. Still standing, I screamed out "those fucking rats!" They laughed like crazy. So, then we examined the mosquito netting and found a small hole where the rat had chewed through and a much bigger hole where I exited. Some of the rats over there were the size of cats. You always wondered what would happen if you were to get bit by one.

"The rats made us so mad that we decided to do something about it. I mentioned taking the bullet out of the jacket of an M-16 round, so we did. Then we packed the end with soap as hard as we could. Next, in the dark, one guy held a rifle loaded with our new soap bullets and one guy with a flashlight. They would then lay on their cots and open fire. It worked perfectly; the rats died in their tracks. Then we would all laugh and laugh. I guess that was just one of the little ways that we would try to relieve our stress because we knew that all too soon, we would be back in the jungle and the rubber trees."

———————

"Had we known that the locals actually harvested rats for food, we could have turned our rats into cash! Many people in tropical Asia would agree. Rats are a popular source of protein in this part of the world, particularly among Vietnamese farming communities in both the north and south. In fact, in the Mekong Delta today, rodent meat fetches higher prices than chicken. Grant Singleton, a scientist who studies ecological rodent management at the International Rice Research Institute in the Philippines, observed that the Mekong Delta alone produces up to 3,600 tons of live rats a year, at a value of about $2 million."

Food vendor
Image Credit: HOANG DINH NAM/AFP via
Getty Images

Tom Pisapia

Shit

"Your day was always full at the Fire Base. If you weren't filling sandbags, it might be your time to be toasting waste with diesel fuel at the latrine. This ritual was performed using 55-gallon drums cut in half and made KP look like a pleasure."

After exhaustive research on the subject of waste disposal in the military, the following narrative was discovered and may be the most authoritative piece ever written on this subject. The article was posted on Vietnamsoldier.com titled "A Year of my Life, Burning Shit: A How to Dispose of Waste Instructional," by Chris Woelk, with photo credit to Randy Barnes.

"Burning Shit: A How to Dispose of Waste Instructional"

Within this story lies one of the many ironies of my tour. Our human waste was valuable to the Vietnamese, and we were burning it.

Burning our shit actually deprived local farmers of valuable fertilizer, used large amounts of gasoline and diesel fuel, served as punishment duty and fouled the Vietnamese sky with a dense, dark black smoke. In Vietnam, human waste was a staple fertilizer. Ours was much richer than that of locals, and each of us out-produced even the best-fed farmer. We could have auctioned it off and made some cash for Uncle Sam or simply given it away.

In base camps, it was a paid job for the Vietnamese, but at fire support bases it was assigned to some poor GI who was out of favor with someone in power. When it came to burning our shit, I think you will, like me, not know whether to laugh or cry, probably both.

To start, the place where we deposited our waste was creative but a sight, I seriously doubt you would ever want to see. It would make an outhouse look like the Taj Mahal. It consisted of two stacks of wood ammo boxes, filled with sand or dirt and placed at each end with a door laid flat across them. Underneath this door were parts of 55-gallon metal drums to catch what fell through the three holes into them. This lovely facility was located out in the open, as were we, sometimes sharing our exposure with "company" at the next hole.

What may seem even more unusual—or horrific depending on your privacy issues—was that we didn't care if we had an audience. When you are in a combat setting, your priorities change significantly. There were way too many serious things to worry about, like being target practice for the enemy there and any other open place. And, even if things were relatively calm, when you live in close quarters in bunkers, privacy becomes an afterthought.

Burning shit was a constant issue, as one side effect of the pills we took made our visits very fluid and frequent if you get my drift. Our food, anti-malaria pills and native bacteria conspired together so that each man, in a firebase averaging 140-200 men, had diarrhea most days. It was a very popular place, creating a significant amount of waste. Pulling these waste-laden cans from under the "thinking platform" slopped the contents around and often onto the person pulling them. The cans to be burned would be half full of a dense liquid with floating solids and a layer of scum at the bottom. The burn location needed to be away from what we fondly called the crapper, so heat from the fire did not stop others from answering nature's call, many of which were emergencies.

The process of burning our shit required us to use empty replacement cans, heavy rubber gloves, the aforementioned gasoline and diesel fuel, some long stir sticks and a stick wrapped with toilet paper on one end, long enough to ignite the mix from a safe distance. Too much gasoline in the combustion mix could toss the contents a good distance when ignited—never a good thing. Everything had to be present and right to excel at this job!

Anyway, before one of the cans was put under the door, some diesel fuel was added to dampen the odor, repel flies and allow the crap to marinate in a combustible liquid. The diesel soaked into the solids and made the next burn go faster. Once ignited in the actual burn stage of the process, the mixture was stirred, and more diesel fuel added as the fire lessoned; gasoline was very dangerous to add but necessary at times. The burning cans also needed to be spaced far enough apart to allow a cool space to move around while stirring. Time passed slowly, and it seemed the contents would never burn away, but hours later a dark, dry residue would be all that remained. After the can cooled, the contents were dumped into a hole and covered. Everyone on that duty knew that a change of clothes and a shower were a must before being welcomed by others.

Like many things in Vietnam, the two-to-four-hour job of burning was weather dependent. Rain, of course, slowed the burn, while wind could whip the smoke up. But it was a no-win situation because if it were too calm, the smoke hovered over the base. Its black particles clung to anything they touched, especially the lucky GI burning it, and its odor was horrific. If it were a calm, clear day, you could *look around and see this highly adhesive black smoke rising from three to eight other fire-bases simultaneously. If there were any kind of breeze, even a light one, the smoke that didn't attach itself to us would fill the sky.*

Men not on burn detail, including enlisted or big-shot officers, seldom came close, so it was an escape in a crazy sort of way. Social stigma was written all over this detail for very sound reasons, but it actually provided a time to be alone and not be instructed (harassed) by leadership (lifers). Some men turned it into an all-day work detail.

Not all of us desired it, however, because many problems happened with this detail, and one of the worst was when the cans were filled too close to the top. This meant part of the contents needed to be poured into an empty can, and the only grip was near the handholds cut near the top of the can. There was no way to avoid having your face very close to this smelly treasure, and any rapid movement set off tidal waves of overflow that landed—yes—right where you are think-

ing. And, you needed to keep the stir stick in motion to prevent it lighting on fire. Being assigned this detail was not a good thing; it was a hot job in a very hot country.

Our artillery was on call 24/7 and a fire mission would bring work details to a stop, at which point the two main jobs became shooting the guns and getting fused 105mm rounds ready and in place at each howitzer. The immediate, overriding priority on any day was fire support and protection, whether it was for those in the field or ourselves. The burning cans were left on their own, along with other daily tasks—they no longer mattered.

As an aside, for the other half of our human waste, we urinated into fiber shipping tubes (piss tubes) that came with each 105mm howitzer round and stuck in a dirt pile. We had several located around the FSB. This system was to reduce the volume of water to be burned off and keep the men from urinating where they stood. At least we could say that between the two bodily functions, we did what we could to reuse and recycle!

Photo credit: Randy Barnes

Credit to Chris Woelk

Tom Pisapia

CHAPTER 8

Fire Fight One

Mid-January 1968

"While in support of the 101st Airborne and the 1st Cavalry Division, we would set up our searchlight that was mounted on a jeep right next to a Quad .50-caliber machine gun mounted on a deuce and a half truck. Most of our free time was spent filling sandbags to put in front of our vehicles for protection against the Viet Cong. Many a night we would sit in the pitch-black jungle and rubber trees waiting for them to crawl up on us to engage. We were hot, sweaty, and constantly swatting mosquitoes while we tried to hold our infra-red binoculars in one hand and operate the searchlight with the other. There was a purr from the jeep running to keep the batteries charged up.

"The infantry would send out scouts to sit in the jungle and listen for the VC. When they spotted or heard them, they would run back toward us and say in a whisper, 'Here they come.' That's when all hell would break loose. The ground trip flares were ignited, and an aerial flare launched, which hung from the sky by parachutes. The open fire was deafening, with every fifth round being a tracer. It looked like a steady stream of red coming out of the Quad 50s. The adrenaline was a rush that I will never forget. We were scared but totally focused on what was in front of us.

"We were always on guard, always alert. The Viet Cong would like to crawl up on our position from about ten p.m. until about four a.m. This still gave them enough time to escape back to where they came from before daybreak. Sneaky little bastards! Next morning it was the same old BS—clean up the bodies, which was done by the infantry. I loved those guys, but we all had our jobs to do. I know that all this seems very senseless, but we were fighting so we could return to our loved ones back home.

"A few weeks later my friends on the Quad 50 went to help a nearby village where the infantry had hit a hot spot. They got shot up and were helicoptered out. I heard they survived, but it was a very sad day; great guys."

——————

This would be the first of what would seem to be an unending pattern of firefights during the rotating two-day journeys into the rubber trees outside of Fire Base Buttons, encroaching into the Viet Cong habitat.

What Dean didn't know, and perhaps no one knew, was what the VC and NVA were planning. It is possible that the upper levels of the US intelligence channels knew what the enemy was planning, but that surely would not be shared with the frontline GIs for a long time.

The Viet Cong were about to launch the largest military campaign of the Vietnam War and it would be considered the turning point in the war. Less than two weeks after Dean's first firefight described above on January 30, 1968, the Tet Offensive began and would continue through September 23, 1968. It would engulf scores of cities, towns, and hamlets throughout Vietnam.

CHAPTER 9

The Tet Offensive and Medics

January 30, 1968

The Tet Offensive was officially called The General Offensive and Uprising of Tet Mau Than 1968 and launched by the Viet Cong and North Vietnamese People's Army of Vietnam against the forces of the South Vietnamese Army of the Republic of Vietnam, the US Armed Forces, and their allies.

It was a campaign of surprise attacks against military and civilian command and control centers throughout South Vietnam. The name of the offensive comes from the Tet holiday, the Vietnamese New Year, when the first major attacks took place.

The offensive was launched prematurely in the late night hours on the January 30, 1968, in the I and II Corps Tactical Zones of South Vietnam. This early attack allowed South Vietnamese and US forces some time to prepare defensive measures. When the main North Vietnamese operation began the next morning, the offensive was countrywide and well-coordinated; eventually more than eighty thousand North Vietnamese and Viet Cong troops struck more than one hundred towns and cities, including thirty-six of forty-four provincial capitals, five of the six autonomous cities, seventy-two of 245 district towns, and the southern capital. The offensive was the largest military operation conducted by either side up to that point in the war.

Hanoi had launched the offensive in the belief that the offensive would trigger a popular uprising leading to the collapse of the South Vietnamese government. Although the initial attacks stunned both the US and South Vietnamese armies, causing them to lose control of several cities temporarily, they quickly regrouped, beat back the attacks, and inflicted heavy casualties on the North Vietnamese and Viet Cong forces. The popular uprising anticipated by Hanoi never happened.

The Battle of Hue began on January 31, 1968, and lasted a total of twenty-six days, resulting in the destruction of the city. During their occupation, the North Vietnamese executed thousands of people in the Massacre at Hue. During the months and years that followed, dozens of mass graves were discovered in and around Hue. Victims included women, men, children, and infants. The estimated death toll was between 2,800 and 6,000 civilians and prisoners of war, or 5 to 10 percent of the total population of Hue.

The Republic of Vietnam released a list of 4,062 victims identified as having been either murdered or abducted. Victims were found bound, tortured, and sometimes buried alive. Many victims were also clubbed to death.

Around the US combat base at Khe Sanh, fighting continued for two more months. The offensive was a military defeat for North Vietnam, though General Westmoreland reported that defeating the North Vietnamese and Viet Cong would require two hundred thousand more American soldiers and activation of the Reserves, prompting even loyal supporters of the war to see that the current war strategy required reevaluation.

The offensive had a strong effect on the US government and shocked the US public, which had been led to believe by its political and military leaders that the North Vietnamese were being defeated and incapable of launching such an ambitious military operation. American public support for the war soon declined and the United States sought negotiations to end the war.

The term "Tet Offensive" usually refers to the January–February 1968 offensive, but it can also include the so-called "Mini-Tet" offensive that took place in May and the Phase III Offensive in August, or the twenty-one weeks of unusually intense combat that followed the initial attacks in January.

Phase II of the Tet Offensive of 1968 (also known as the May Offensive, Little Tet, and Mini-Tet) was launched by the People's Army of Vietnam and Viet Cong against targets throughout South Vietnam, including Saigon from April 29 to May 30, 1968. The May Offensive was considered much bloodier than the initial phase of the Tet Offensive.

US casualties across South Vietnam were 2,169 killed for the entire month of May, making it the deadliest month of the entire Vietnam War for US forces, while South Vietnamese losses were 2,054 killed. PAVN/VC losses exceeded 24,000 killed and over 2,000 captured. The May Offensive was a costly defeat for the PAVN/VC.

However, the deadliest week of the Vietnam War for the United States was during the initial phase of the Tet Offensive, specifically February 11–17, 1968, during which 543 Americans were killed in action and 2,547 were wounded.

The number of wounded had doubled during the Tet Offensive and put a tremendous strain on the combat medics and their resources. The battlefield medical treatment is critical to the survival of the wounded. Numbers show that if the wounded can survive the first twenty-four hours after their injury, they have a 99 percent chance of survival.

Combat medics courageously fought to save lives as the war raged around them in Vietnam. Helicopters became virtual hospitals in the air, buying the combat medic valuable time to heal the wounded. When lives were on the line, it was a combat medic's quick thinking that determined the fate of their fellow troop.

Medics carried green pouches stuffed to the brim with abdominal dressings (large bandages), battle dressings (medium-sized dressings), four to five rolls of gauze, and five to ten morphine syrettes.

Tom Pisapia

Medic Flashbacks

Beloved by their fellow grunts, corpsmen and medics are the first responders for Marines and soldiers wounded on the battlefield. Here are the firsthand accounts of decorated "Docs" who provided life-saving aid in Vietnam.

The scene could have come from the movies. May 21, 1969: Nineteen-year-old Navy Hospital Corpsman Michael Kuklenski was three weeks deep into his Vietnam tour—on patrol with Alpha Co., 1st Bn., 7th Marines, 1st Marine Div., when he heard a land mine go off. Almost simultaneously, he saw something tumble over his head. It was a boot, and in it, part of a lower leg.

"Corpsman up!" came the yell. Three men were down, one of them dead. They lay across an open field. Kuklenski started out across it to render aid. Already there was the company's senior corpsman, Jim Goss.

One of the surviving Marines, a former athlete, had lost both legs below the knees. Goss and Kuklenski tied off what was left to stop the bleeding, then administered morphine.

Suddenly, the critically wounded Marine broke into song. It was his birthday. "He's singing Happy Birthday," said Kuklenski, a VFW Department of Texas member and retired businessman in suburban Dallas. "I'm trying to save his life...and keep some composure."

A week later the conscientious objector corpsman's composure would be put to the ultimate test.

May 29, 1969: Alpha Company set an ambush for North Vietnamese Army regulars, thirty of whom had been using a trail on a regular basis. Unbeknownst to the Marines, the NVA saw this and countered with an ambush of their own. Instead of the usual thirty NVA, more than three times that many showed up.

"They pretty much wiped out our unit," Kuklenski said. Seventy percent of those in his unit were killed or wounded. Kuklenski was one of them. He was hit three separate times, incurring wounds to both arms and both legs.

Unable to walk, the powerful fireplug of a man (a former star guard on the Dallas Jesuit High School football team) pulled himself along with his elbows, treating the wounded as he went, remembering all along the mantra of corpsmen and medics alike: Clear the airway, stop the bleeding, prevent or treat for shock.

His deeds earned him the Silver Star.

According to US Navy Bureau of Medicine and Surgery historian Andre Sobocinski, more than ten thousand Navy hospital corpsmen served with Marines during Vietnam. Of those, 645 were killed in action and more than 3,300 wounded.

Sanders Marble, PhD, is senior historian, History Branch, of the US Army's Medical Department Center of History and Heritage at Fort Sam Houston in San Antonio, Texas. He said, "There are no clear statistics on how many [Army] medics were deployed to Vietnam."

There are, however, clear stats as to how many medical personnel in Vietnam were awarded the nation's highest commendation for bravery. According to the Medal of

Honor Society, 259 medals were conferred for actions during the Vietnam War. Twenty of them went to medics, corpsmen, and the like—one out of every thirteen conferred.

Courage, composure, and guardian angels like Kuklenski were part and parcel of Jess Johnson's medic kit.

Johnson was eighteen when he deployed as a medic with A Co., 1st Bn., 501st Inf. Regt., 101st Airborne Division. Courage was instilled in him by his father, a soldier with the 78th Lightning Division who lost a leg during the Battle of the Bulge in WWII. One day, Johnson's father took him aside and said, "You have to be in combat to be a man." As a result, the son volunteered to go to Vietnam.

"Because of my naivete," Johnson said, "I didn't believe that I could ever get hurt."

Time would put the Bronze Star and two-time Purple Heart recipient's belief to the test—illustrating the importance of courage, composure, and faith.

Johnson's experience in combat taught him that a wounded patient's perception can tip the person into shock, a state of affairs that can lead to death. He believes a medic must give his or her patients hope. Johnson's technique was to make a wounded soldier laugh by saying something like, "I can't believe that you're going home and I have to stay here."

"If I could make my patient laugh a little bit and give him hope that he's going to see his wife and brand-new baby," he said, "that would usually increase survivability by fifty percent. You never, ever want to say, 'My God, man, I don't know if I can save you.'"

There is a strange relationship between battlefield patient and combat medic or hospital corpsman, one of intimate detachment. Life and limb, you hold another human being's fate in your hands.

"I never talked to them again after I 'medevac'd' them," Johnson said. "I didn't know if they lived or died. I did the best I could."

It is this kind of composure that helped Johnson survive eleven months in Vietnam, many of them around the murderous A Shau Valley.

Sept. 11, 1971: Four members of 2nd

Platoon were hit early in the day in an NVA ambush. Johnson and the M60 gunner set off to find them and render aid. At the time, he didn't realize he would exhaust his day's medical supplies treating them.

Later that day, the platoon leader dispatched Johnson and another man down a sloping hill to a grassy area. The day was typical for the A Shau: no wind, dead calm, and hot as hell. And yet patches of the grass were moving.

"I look up and there's this air vent, in the middle of no place," Johnson said. He had stumbled across an NVA command bunker.

Johnson called his platoon leader. The lieutenant said a fire mission was about to be called in from the USS New Jersey. Thirty minutes later, its massive rounds began to fall. As he ran back up the hill for shelter, Johnson stepped into a fire ant mound. He bent over, yanking to free his foot.

"As I'm bending over, I hear a whoosh!" he remembered.

It was a large, lethal piece of one of the

New Jersey's rounds. Had he been standing he would have been decapitated.

———————

Combat medics in the Navy trained for sixteen weeks of Hospital Corps School. Then an additional three weeks in Field Medical School, learning how to operate with the Marines. Comparatively, the Army spent only eight weeks training their Vietnam medics, half the time the Navy devoted.

"Their brothers' keepers: Medics & corpsmen in Vietnam"
By Jerome Greer Chandler, VFW Magazine / Published January 11, 2018

"VFW member Jerome Greer Chandler was an Army medic, a 91A. In 1970 he served with D Co., 2nd Bn., 501st Inf. Regt., 101st Airborne Div. A regular contributor to *VFW magazine*, Chandler is a former assistant professor at Jacksonville State University in Alabama.

Medics SP4 Gerald Levy and Pfc. Andrew J. Brown with a wounded soldier and a paratrooper of the 173rd Airborne Brigade, Bien Hoa, Vietnam. (Photo by Horst Faas)

Tom Pisapia

CHAPTER 10

Mountain Yards

"We would see the Mountain Yard tribes on occasion. However, they were usually in the company of the Army Special Forces or Green Berets. It was their mission to wage guerrilla warfare and organize resistance behind enemy lines. The Green Berets were training them to get information about troop movement in the Central Highlands and the Ho Chi Minh Trail.

"The Mountain Yard was a tribe that used bow and arrows and blowguns for killing monkeys and birds for food high above them in the trees. They wore very little clothes in the jungle and their women were often seen naked from the waist up. They were trained and then outfitted with rifles. Crazy stuff!"

A Montagnard tribesman during training in 1962.

As far back as the eighth century, long before the Chinese Oriental Vietnamese arrived in Vietnam, the "Montagnard" Degar tribes were there. There were twenty to twenty-eight tribes of ethnic minorities who looked like Polynesian people and spoke a language similar to Polynesian. The French gave them the name "Montagnard," a carryover from the French protectorate period in Vietnam, which meant "mountain-dweller." The Americans soldiers mispronounced the word Montagnard and named them "Mountain Yards," which was then shorten to "Yards." The Mountain Yards refer to themselves as "Dega."

They are the indigenous peoples of the Central Highlands of Vietnam. In 1962, the population of the Degar people in the Central Highlands was estimated to number as many as one million.

As the Vietnam War began to loom on the horizon, both South Vietnamese and American policymakers sought to begin training troops from minority groups in the Vietnamese populace. The US Mission to Saigon sponsored the training of the Degar in unconventional warfare by American Special Forces. These newly trained Degar were seen as a potential ally in the Central Highlands area to stop Viet Cong activity in the region and a means of preventing further spread of Viet Cong sympathy.

Later, their participation would become much more important as the Ho Chi Minh Trail, the North Vietnamese supply line for Viet Cong forces in the south, grew. The US military, particularly the Special Forces, developed base camps in the area and recruited the Degar. Because of their quiet resolve and skills in tracking, roughly forty thousand fought alongside American soldiers and became a major part of the US military effort in the Highlands and I Corps, the northernmost region of South Vietnam.

In 1967, the Viet Cong killed and incinerated 252 Degar including old men, women, and young children in the village of Dak Son, home to two thousand Highlanders, known as the Dak Son massacre, in revenge for the Degar's support and allegiance with South Vietnam.

In 1975, thousands of Degar fled to Cambodia after the fall of Saigon to the North Vietnamese Army, fearing that the new government would launch reprisals against them because they had aided the US Army. The US

Tom Pisapia

military resettled some Degar in the United States, primarily in North Carolina, but these evacuees numbered less than two thousand. In addition, the Vietnamese government has steadily displaced thousands of villagers from Vietnam's Central Highlands, to use the fertile land for coffee plantations.

The French colonized the Degars (Yards) and were good and generous to them and did not try to change them. The Yards really liked the French. The Jesuit French missionaries were also good to the Yards, and after twelve years of influence, 80 percent of the Yards became Catholic, and by the 1930s, 20 percent became Protestant.

Before the Vietnam War, they lived in the uninhabited mountains of the Central Highlands. They were nomadic, and some of their hooches (huts) were built on stilts to keep animals from wandering into the homes. There was mutual hatred for the Yards by the North and South Vietnamese. The Vietnamese called the Yards "MOI," which meant "savage." It was said that the South Vietnamese Air

Force had an understanding that if any bombs were left over from bombing raids, they were to be dropped on the Yard villages.

Since the Yards didn't like the Vietnamese, the French used this to their advantage as a counterinsurgency. The French taught them how to use modern weapons, but many Yards still preferred the crossbows and spears especially when foraging the jungle for food. They were good hunters and farmers. In 1962, when the American Special Forces arrived in Vietnam the Yards liked them also. Perhaps it was because they were tall and looked similar to the French with their green berets. The Army Green Berets were also good to the Yards and taught them to use the M-1 carbines. "The Yards gave their lives to save Green Berets, and Green Berets did likewise." The Yards were part of the 5th Mobile Strike Force which was a quick reaction force to protect besieged camps and were especially helpful along the Ho Chi Minh Trail.

The Yards generally wore brightly colored cavalry scarves given by the Green Berets so that companies could quickly distinguish their Yards from other company Yards. Most Yards wore jungle fatigues when out on fighting jungle missions; when off-duty, they wore their tribal dress, which was as little clothing as possible, similar to loin cloths. The Yards were often seen wearing cast-off clothing, which was ragged and always dirty. They generally had bracelets and beads and medicine packets worn on leather string necklaces. For bullet protection they wore Buddha medallions to ward off any Buddhist bullets, because they believed that all Vietnamese soldiers were Buddhist, while in reality most were atheists.

The Yards have been described as childlike in their enthusiasm for life by always smiling and being happy. They looked tough but horsed around like juveniles. By the same token, they were fierce warriors. Although a simple, primitive people, who saw things as good or bad, black and white, with few shades of gray, they were also good scouts. The Yards were in tune to jungle sounds and could tell if people were nearby listening to the sounds that the animals and insects made. In the jungle they were never without food, because they could pick up things such as leaves, bugs, berries, and lizards to eat in their rice bowl. Like the American Indians, the Yards saw their world as alive, with spirits dwelling in everything including inanimate objects.

Most Yards had never seen electricity back then and were really excited about the movies. The American military compounds would show movies on projection screens. The first time the Yards saw the movie *The Good, The Bad, and The Ugly*, they shot up the screen. They especially liked cowboy movies but couldn't separate the real world from the movie world. The military would end up using bed sheets or bleach mosquito netting as a screen. To protect people who might be walking behind the movie screens, they would set up plywood and sandbags. The Yards loved action movies but didn't understand technology and were very superstitious.

In some special friendships or warrior recognition, the Yards would offer the Americans membership in their tribes, which was considered an honor. Their blood brother ritual consisted of drinking rice wine and christening the person with his new tribal name. The new blood brother would then be given a brass bracelet, which was never to be removed. Their superstitions held that removing this bracelet meant bad luck.

John Wayne made a movie, *The Green Berets,* which used some of the Yards in the film. The Rhade tribe in 1967 gave him a brass bracelet that he never removed. The bracelet was seen in his later movies, and he supposedly was buried with the bracelet on.

The American military felt that the Yards were trustworthy, and they proved their loyalty by protecting our military. On one occasion, the Yards brought two American pilots to the 67th Evacuation Hospital. The pilots had been shot down and sent to a prison camp as POWs, where they were rescued by the Yards. The South Vietnamese military hospitals would not treat wounded Yard fighters. The civilian hospitals treated the Yards as second-class citizens and offered little help to their families. The 67th Evacuation Hospital and other American medical facilities were basically their only source of medical care.

After the war, the Vietnamese government practiced genocide against the Yards. Those Yards remaining in Vietnam after the fall of Saigon were called spies and traitors for helping the Americans. They could not wear their traditional clothing or speak their languages on the streets for fear of being beaten by the Vietnamese communities. The young children were not permitted education beyond the fifth grade. The Vietnamese government displaced thousands of villagers from their lands and turned their ancestral forests into coffee-growing plantations. The Yards have continually sought help from the international communities.

The Green Berets have established a non-profit charity called "Save the Montagnard People." By 2008, along with the help of the

State Department, human rights groups, and churches, the Green Berets sponsored eight to nine thousand Yards. They settled them in the Triad area of North Carolina (between Greensboro, Raleigh, and Charlotte). The Green Berets have procured 101 acres for their use.

In addition, they have built long houses for Yard ceremonies that are open to the public twice a year on Memorial Day and in September on a Yard holiday. Crafts such as colorful blankets and brass bracelets from the Mountain Yards still living in Vietnam are smuggled out and sold to tourists. During the Vietnam War, there were seven million Mountain Yards; in 2014 there were only six hundred thousand left. The Green Berets have not forgotten the help the Yards gave them during the Vietnam War and are doing their best to ensure that the Montagnard culture lives on.

CHAPTER 11

Fire Fight Two and Agent Orange

Late January 1968

"In late January '68, I was still with I Battery, 29th Artillery attached to the 101st Airborne at Fire Base Buttons. I was again operating my searchlight next to a Quad .50-caliber machine gun on a deuce and a half truck when we were in a firefight with the VC. After the firefight, the 101st would drag the VC bodies and lay them against the rubber trees and would stick the 101st patch in their chests. Their bodies were charred beyond recognition. We would spend two nights in the jungle and then two nights at the fire base, guarding the perimeter. The firebase had eight-inch guns and 175 mm guns that would fire H&I all night long to keep the enemy at bay and keep mortar and rocket attacks down.

"While at the Fire Base, you would sleep underground in bunkers that had railroad ties and sandbags on the ceilings. When you woke up from a rare cat nap, you could not recognize your face due to the red clay that would seep through the ceiling day and night due to the firing of the big guns. Because of the spraying of Agent Orange and the constant rain, it was nothing but red clay and red mud. The place was overrun with rats and snakes and bugs."

Dean with the sandbags and ammo cans
that framed his bunker

Agent Orange was a tactical herbicide used by the US military from 1962 to 1971, named for the orange identifying stripe used on the 55-gallon drums in which it was stored.

The military sprayed millions of gallons of Agent Orange and other tactical herbicides on trees and vegetation during the Vietnam War for the dual purpose of defoliating forest areas that might conceal Viet Cong and North Vietnamese forces and destroying crops that might feed the enemy.

The US launched the spraying of Agent Orange on January 18, 1962. After a period of testing, on this day in 1962, President John F. Kennedy gave final approval to "Operation Ranch Hand"—a massive effort to defoliate the forests of Vietnam, Cambodia, and Laos with an herbicide known as Agent Orange.

During the Vietnam War, the US military sprayed nearly twenty million gallons of various chemicals—the "rainbow herbicides" and defoliants as part of the aerial defoliation program. By far, Agent Orange was the combination the US military used most often.

Heavy sprayed areas included forests near the demarcation zone; forests at the junction of the borders of Cambodia, Laos, and South Vietnam; and mangroves on the southernmost peninsula of Vietnam and along shipping channels southeast of Saigon.

The US Department of Defense developed these tactical herbicides specifically to be used in "combat operations." They were not commercial-grade herbicides purchased from chemical companies and sent to Vietnam. Tactical herbicides also were used, tested, and stored in areas outside of Vietnam.

The dioxin TCDD was an unwanted byproduct of herbicide production. Dioxins are pollutants released into the environment by burning waste, diesel exhaust, chemical manufacturing, and other processes. TCDD is the most toxic of the dioxins and classified as a human carcinogen by the Environmental Protection Agency.

Agent Orange dries quickly after spraying and breaks down within hours to days when exposed to sunlight (if not bound chemically to a biological surface such as soil, leaves, and grass) and is no longer harmful.

From 1965 to 1969, the former Monsanto Company manufactured Agent Orange for the US military as a wartime government contractor. The current Monsanto Company has maintained responsibility for this product since it was spun off as a separate, independent agricultural company in 2002.

Veterans who may have been exposed to Agent Orange include those who were in Vietnam, the Korean Demilitarized Zone, on Thai Air Force bases, and who flew on or worked on C-123 Aircraft. Several decades later, concerns about the health effects from these chemicals, including dioxin, a byproduct of Agent Orange production, continue.

The VA offers eligible veterans a free Agent Orange Registry health exam for possible long-term health problems related to exposure. The VA also offers health care, disability compensation, and other benefits to eligible veterans for certain disease conditions, as well as benefits for children of Vietnam Veterans who have spina bifida. Dependents and survivors may also be eligible for other benefits.

Rigorous studies have consequently been conducted to measure the levels of dioxin still present in the blood samples of the citizens of both North and South Vietnam. It is estimated that about four hundred thousand Vietnamese were killed by the toxic effects of Agent Orange.

With an estimated 390 Vietnam veterans passing each day, there will be few, if any, alive in just ten years, estimates The American War Library. March 29 is designated each year as National Vietnam Veterans Memorial Day with ceremonies held across the country.

Of the 2,709,918 Americans who served in Vietnam, less than eight hundred fifty thousand were estimated to be alive in 2014. Unfortunately, more current numbers were not available as of this publication. The Vietnam Memorial lists the names of more than fifty-eight thousand Americans who died overseas. However, the wall does not document any names of the estimated 2.8 million US vets who were exposed to the poisonous chemical while serving and later died.

Cancers the VA believes are caused by contact with Agent Orange include:

Tom Pisapia

Chronic B-cell leukemia: A type of cancer that affects the white blood cells.

Hodgkin's disease: A type of cancer that attacks the lymph nodes, liver, and spleen.

Multiple myeloma: A type of cancer that affects plasma cells.

Non-Hodgkin's lymphoma: A group of cancers that affect the lymph nodes.

Prostate cancer: Affects the prostate.

Respiratory cancers including lung cancer.

Soft tissue sarcomas.

AL amyloidosis: A rare illness that happens when an abnormal protein builds up in the body's tissues.

Chloracne: or other types of acneiform disease like it.

Diabetes mellitus type 2: An illness that happens when the body is unable to properly use insulin.

Ischemic heart disease: A type of heart

disease that happens when the heart doesn't get enough blood.

Parkinson's disease: An illness of the nervous system.

Peripheral neuropathy, early onset: An illness of the nervous system that causes numbness, tingling, and weakness.

Porphyria cutanea tarda: A rare illness that can affect normal liver function and can cause the skin to thin and blister when exposed to the sun.

If you have an illness you believe is caused by contact with Agent Orange—and you don't see it listed above, you can still file a claim for disability compensation.

Call MyVA at 844-698-2311
or visit the website:

https://www.va.gov/disability/eligibility/haz-ardous-materials-exposure/agent-orange/related-diseases/

Agent Orange spraying
Jets spraying herbicides in Cambodia
Image Credit: Bettmann / Getty Images

CHAPTER 12

Snakes

"While I was stationed at Song Be Fire Base Buttons, we were under mortar attack. I was operating my searchlight when the attack started. We all headed for the underground bunkers when one of our gunners was bit by a snake. The medic thought it to be deadly, so we called in a medevac helicopter. They flew him away and we didn't know what happened to him."

By far, the best description of what the GIs had to deal with regarding snakes in Vietnam is written by Ray Sarlin below.

100% Alert and Then Some!

"In late 1969, I commanded Delta Company,

1st Battalion (Mechanized), 50th Infantry, 173rd Airborne Brigade in Phan Thiet, Binh Thuan Province, South Vietnam, the nuoc mam capital of the World. Whether by coincidence or design, the province is also home to many varieties of venomous snakes. In fact, Vietnam is home to some of the world's deadliest snakes such as Asian cobras, king cobras, coral snakes, kraits, and numerous vipers and pit vipers.

One snake was called a "Two-step" by GI's, because the word was you could only walk two steps after being bitten before you died. This may have been a myth to keep GI's alert in the bush, because there are no known snakes in the world that can kill that fast. The fastest known killer, Africa's Black Mamba, can kill in about 2-1/2 minutes if bitten directly into a major artery or vein that goes straight to the heart. Generally speaking, though, it takes 15 to 30 minutes before life threatening symptoms appear from a snake bite, and usually a minimum of several hours or even days before death occurs from bites of even very venomous snakes.

But the fact is that over 30 of Vietnam's 140 snake species are poisonous. Even now, about 30,000 people are bitten by snakes in Vietnam every year, and many of them die. So the fact that the term "two-stepper" might be a myth that doesn't mean that snakes shouldn't be treated with respect...and are best avoided whenever possible.

The Army didn't tell us how to tell "good" snakes from "bad" snakes, probably because it fell into the too-hard basket! Maybe they didn't tell us because it would've spoiled the Drill Instructor's best snake joke, "The Nam has a hundred species of snakes: 99 are poisonous and can kill you with a bite; the other one ain't poisonous but will crush you to death!"

In any case, what they didn't seem to want us to know is that if a snake has a round head, round pupils, no fangs, and a double row of plates on the tail, it's probably nonpoisonous (with some exceptions). However, if a snake has a triangular head, huge fangs, elliptical pupils and a single row of plates on its butt, watch out!

See how simple this is? Of course, the cobra is one of the exceptions because it has a round head and round pupils. And the cobra, especially the black Monocellate Cobra (Naja kaouthia) that features in so many GI snake stories, was one bad mutha! Its bite can be fatal within 60 minutes without treatment. Fortunately the majority of cases don't result in such extreme systemic poisoning, the area around the bite simply swells up and the tissue all around dies and you get paralyzed, have trouble breathing, pass out and can die later on.

So maybe a fear of snakes isn't so irrational after all. In particular, fear of the Monocellate Cobra seems quite well-founded, because the snake is known to strike multiple times to inject more and more venom.

Cobras are big snakes, with mature cobras four to eight feet long. The King Cobra, which is in a class by itself, can grow up over 5 meters (17.5 feet) long! Thank God they didn't have King Cobras where I grew up in Arizona, or I'll probably be digested by now. When I worked on the Coconino National Forest before Nam, we experimented with Western Diamondback Rattlers to see if the old wives' tale about snakes biting half their length was true. Since our survey range poles were 8 feet long and the biggest rattler was reputed to be 14 feet long, we had a whole foot of pole to hang on to when we taunted them to strike. With one ten-footer, I mesmerized the snake with the tip of the range pole, and then without warning the triangular head thrust forward and its mouth gripped the pole at the 5-foot mark, fangs oozing poison. Geez, I can't believe how dumb I was back then!

Anyway I lived to become Delta Company Commander in lovely Phan Thiet overlooking the South China Sea. LZ Betty's eastern bunker line was built on top of the sand cliffs over the beach, thus creating a dead spot along the base of the cliffs to suck in the NVA, but other than mortars and a satchel charge or two, things were usually pretty quiet on that side. The assaults tended to come through the cemetery on the other side, because we would sometimes have trouble

Tom Pisapia

getting clearance to fire our weapons there, what with the friendly city of Phan Thiet to the west and northwest.

That's not to say that tower duty on the coastal side was a piece of cake, because it was really just as important as any other side of the Greenline (perimeter). It's just that with the cleared flat sandy ground, our defenses had excellent fields of fire and the claymores were ready for action. On the more populated sides there were always reasonable excuses for Vietnamese civilians to be wandering around in the daytime pacing off distances and observing the defensive positions. On the unpopulated eastern side, anybody seen walking around was likely to receive a whole lot of unwelcome attention.

The net result of all this inequity in guard duty, of course, was that pulling guard duty on the coastal side could actually be kind of pleasant. Each tower had a big bunker on the ground where the relief crew could sleep when not on shift, and the bunkers each had a decent fighting position on the roof that doubled as a sun deck during the day and a great place to watch the brilliant colors of a Southeast Asian sunset reflect off the serene waters of the South China Sea. Of course, the sun actually set behind you unless you were Hamchuk in the film "The Green Berets," but you know what I mean about watching the colors of the sunset on the waters. It was quite peaceful and serene.

But "peacefulness" and serenity were not the prescription for maximum alertness on the Greenline. Quite the opposite, in fact! They were recipes for disaster because they were the prescription for slumber. And that is why Officers and NCOs were created!

As a Company Commander, my job description didn't exactly have me pulling the Officer of the Day inspections of the Greenline bunkers, but Ranger School had taught me to expect the unexpected whenever on the defensive. That lesson was particularly useful in Vietnam! So I would unobtrusively circulate around the Greenline where my men were assigned at night even when I wasn't required to, just as I would later on go around the fighting positions in the field late at night and chat with the troops when the military situation allowed.

The protocol was to use the landline to let people know you were on the prowl, and then approach the bunker on foot by the road. We'd chat a bit with the guys on top of the bunker, and then possibly climb the tower to spend a few pleasant minutes from that vantage point and maybe check things out through the Starlight scope (AN/TVS-5 Crew Served Weapon Night Sight) mounted on the .50 cal machine gun in the tower. I suspect that there would have been a long line for this duty if there had been something like nurses quarters or an apartment block within 1,000 yards, but it was still pleasant to watch the gentle white water of waves in the green light, as well as to check out the occasional water craft outside the line of floating barrels that marked the no-go zone.

As it was, checking the guard gave me a chance to chat informally in a non-threatening environment with the men I was assigned to support and look out for. It was a way to get a feel for that elusive concept "morale", and a chance to exercise a little "leadership." And who knows, you might actually learn something that you needed to know before things blew up in your face. At the very least, you could hear a decent joke or two.

It was probably about 0200 (2 a.m.) one night when I strolled up to the bunker, expecting to chat with one or two guys there and work-out whether or not to climb the ladder. I spotted the tell-tale embers glowing in cupped fists on top of the bunker and walked straight toward the ladder by the bunker door.

'Sir, sir!' I heard urgently hissed down from on high. And then a loud whisper said, "Don't go near the door! There's another ladder on the side. And be quiet!" and another loud whisper said, "Shhhh!" Then several others also said, "Shhhh!"

I stopped and did a double-take...instead of only a few men on the roof of the bunker like I expected, it was everybody on duty other than the man in the tower! My mind was working in overdrive, and in microseconds (nanoseconds weren't invented yet) I thought, "L'see, they're on 100% alert at 0200 and they're whispering! Geez, they must have some enemy in the wire!" Of course, the cigarettes and using the side ladder didn't compute, but there were enough clues to know that we were going to see some action!

"Shhh!" came again, which was a bit rich, I thought. I hadn't so much as breathed out!

I walked over to the side ladder like I had been trained in Ranger School and Jungle School, heel-to-toe, heel-to-toe. I was as stealthy as a black panther stalking its prey. The air around my body was still, undisturbed. And then I reached the ladder and started to climb, slowly, stealthily. There was no school for climbing ladders in combat, but as an experienced Seattle Mountaineer I had mastered the three-point contact rock and ice climbing method, and oozed up the ladder silently, not even casting a shadow in the still evening nautical twilight.

Still someone had the poor form to shush me again before I topped the crest of the sandbagged revetment. I expected to see troops fitted out in flak vests and helmets, weapons pointed downrange beneath keenly alert, narrowed eyes engaged in target acquisition. Instead, it appeared that I had interrupted a poker party, because the hands were laid out on a mortar ammo case with some MPC scattered around. Make no mistake, though, the men were wide awake and alert, so it wouldn't have been a good time to try to palm a card.

"Uh, Captain, we got a visitor downstairs." The story emerged in a rush with most of them talking all at once. It seems that everything had gone along normally, and the relief split up to go their separate way down below into the bunker to get some shuteye, while the duty guards settled in for a normal shift. An alert guard on top of the bunker spotted a large snake heading for the bunker and sounded the alert. Quick as a flash, the position went to 100% alert! Despite that, the

snake went into the bunker and refused to leave...so the men on duty were content to wait until daylight to try to get the snake. Equilibrium reigned on the Greenline until I came along!

When I became aware of the full significance of what I had been told, one of the options that seemed attractive was spending the rest of the night bonding with my troops, but then my little voice suggested that there were better options and that I had a job to do.

I've had quite a bit to do with poisonous snakes in my life, just don't ask me to tell you their scientific names or their mating habits. I've killed 'em and skinned them and eaten them...and even have a personal story about the sighting of the largest ever recorded snake, an Anaconda in the Amazonia region of Brazil which had just finished ingesting a cow. But that's a story for another day. So, I'm not especially afraid of snakes, even large mean ones like we seemed to come across in Vietnam. On the other hand, I'm not reckless around them, either. I have a healthy respect for them, even if it doesn't work both ways. In the end, when my heartbeat returned to normal after working out who was shushing me, I decided to regain the initiative and go look for Joe Snake so that the life of my troops could return to normal.

With a red-filtered flashlight, I peered over the sand-bagged parapets and confirmed that the snake was either still inside the bunker or had escaped under the wire and was hopefully terrifying any sappers that were reconnoitering the LZ. The coast was clear as I retraced my steps back down the ladder and then walked around to the bunker entrance, my left hand holding my red flashlight out in front like you see in police movies these days, with my M16 ready to unload on any creature unlucky enough to encounter me that night.

Finally, I was facing the black rectangle that led into the dark, foreboding bunker. Nothing stirred. I moved closer to the opening, shining my light ahead and then took another step. Suddenly there was a flash of red several feet off the floor as the light reflected back at me...and then another reddish flash...and then the outline of an alerted cobra slowly emerged from the darkness. He had me in his sights, and he knew it!

The sinewy creature was swaying softly, tongue flicking past his ready fangs, waiting for a taste, - for a banquet - of human flesh. Give him his tiny moment of fantasy, I thought, it will help for him to become overconfident.

Time for me to size him up. He appeared to be over two meters long which immediately posed a problem, because that was double the length of my M16 rifle, eliminating my trusty Arizona trick used with so many rattlesnakes. Although cobras are reputed to be relatively slow on the ground, their strike is as fast as lightning.

Still, all of my old snake experience could still be put to good use, and I noticed that the cobra's fearsome head undulated in synch with the rhythm of my quavering M16's flash suppresser. "Hmmm", I thought. "I wonder *if...." Sure enough, the cobra seemed to have a death wish or else was supremely self-confident, because it kept the barrel of my weapon pointed right at its head. I gently shifted the muzzle back and forth and sure enough he swayed in time with it. Ah, here was my enemy's fatal weakness, the flaw that would see to its demise.*

Shifting my rifle to my left hand while keeping the cobra mesmerized, I slowly unholstered my trusty .45 caliber pistol, this particular snake hunter's weapon of choice. I could imagine the crafty beast dodging a spinning .556 round or, worse yet, having it blast through him like a hot knife through butter to make him really angry, but I couldn't see even the hardiest snake shaking off a .45 round in the kisser. The problem, of course, was getting one in his kisser, but it looked like the snake himself would help compensate for any aiming error on my part.

Now the task was to shift his attention from barrel of the M16 to the business end of the .45. I would lose one advantage of the M16, maintaining the distance between us. Another advantage of the M16 I would lose was the ability to spray a magazine on full automatic at him if he attacked and then run like hell. A further disadvantage of the .45 was that if a slug actually hit the snake, there would be a need for a good cleanup before the bunker was again habitable. Still, these disadvantages were outweighed by the pistol's stopping power.

So I moved to Plan B. Plan B was to lure the snake out of the bunker and either nail his butt outside of the bunker or wave Aloha as he slithered off to the east. This meant using all my cunning to fool the snake into thinking that I was removing his remaining obstacle to freedom (myself) while luring him into the killing zone outside the bunker. Heck, this strategy had worked well with skunks when I was in the Forest Service, when we used to herd them with flashlights into the tents of campers who gave us problems.

In this case, Plan B meant slowly moving back and to the right, turning my body's center of mass so that I continued to face the alerted cobra. It worked, and he started moving forward cautiously out of the bunker and to my left, getting ready for his dash to cover. I started moving with him to keep him cautious and forestall his sprint to safety. Everything was going according to plan.

Then to my right as I passed the bunker doorway, eyes focused to my front on the escaping cobra, I heard a "Shhhh!" coming from the bunker. I must have jumped so high that I could've stepped onto the top of the bunker. Quickly reverting to Plan A for Snake B, I unleashed a withering fire from my .45 into the hapless second cobra.

Actually, the cleanup wasn't as bad as anticipated. My only regret is that the first one got away; perhaps the moral of this story is to never look a gift snake in the mouth."

CHAPTER 13

Jeeps and Mortars

"After spending a night in the rubber trees, two other troops and I had to go back to base camp for gas and supplies. On the way back, the VC had dropped a couple of mortars in our area. The driver of my Jeep stepped on the gas as fast as the Jeep would go. I was sitting on the back fender of the jeep when he hit a pothole and threw me in the air; my helmet and M-16 went flying. I can remember coming down on the ground and I was pretty banged up. What was weird is when I sat up, a second lieutenant was there and asked me, 'Are you okay, soldier?' I replied, 'I think so.' I don't know where he came from, but I looked around, all I could see was him and my Jeep, heading down the road without me. The guys finally realized that I was no longer on the jeep and came back and got my sorry ass—just another day in that hellhole."

The mortar rounds that spooked the Jeep driver and left Dean dazed and bruised on the cratered roadside were an all too familiar event in the Vietnam War. Both the NVA and the VC were quite adept at using mortars at not only quick strikes on American installations but also for their own style of H&I fire.

Let's take a closer look into this relatively unsophisticated weapon that has been used in wars since 1673. Many countries since then have made improvements to the basic mortar including the United States, France, England, and others over the years. The forerunner of the present-day mortar was designed by the British and used in World War I in 1915.

Each mortar shell had a screw-on cap in its base. Inside the hollow in the tail, it contained a 20-gauge M5A1 Ignition Cartridge. This was a paper shotgun shell filled with ballistite powder. Ballistite is a smokeless propellant made from two high explosives, nitrocellulose and nitroglycerine. It was developed and patented by Alfred Nobel in 1887.

The mortar had a firing pin in the bottom of the tube. When the shell was dropped down the tube, the firing pin struck the ignition cartridge in the shell's tail, detonating it. When the cartridge detonated, the explosive gases exited the base of the shell through two bleed holes. This propelled the shell out of the tube in an arc. Unassisted, the mortar shell had a range of about 200 to 325 yards.

As a muzzle-loading weapon, the operator need only drop the mortar projectile down the mouth of the tube and protect himself from the subsequent launch blast. This method of operation allowed the mortar crew to supply a steady rate of accurate firepower in support of infantry operations before them. A trained crew could effectively fire off eighteen rounds in a minute and reach ranges from one hundred yards out to two thousand yards, with each projectile maintaining a possible seventeen to thirty-five foot blast

Tom Pisapia

radius or "kill zone." A maximum rate-of-fire by a trained crew could reach thirty to thirty-five rounds-per-minute while extreme circumstances state a rate per minute of one hundred rounds!

Although the US and SVA used a number of different mortars, the most popular was the 60mm M2 mortar. It was easy to transport at only 42.5 pounds, had a range of 77 to 3,825 yards (2.17 miles), a blast radius of about twenty-five yards depending on the mortar shell used, and was usually operated by a crew of three soldiers, though it was possible for one soldier to operate the weapon.

US M2 60mm mortar

Mortars are not especially accurate weapons. The first round may be one hundred meters or more off-target, but by adjusting the aim point, the crew can get on target after a few shots.

Mortars are fired for various reasons, such as lighting up targets with illumination mortar cartridges, destroying targets with high-explosive ammunition mortar rounds, or firing white phosphorous smoke rounds.

Tom Pisapia

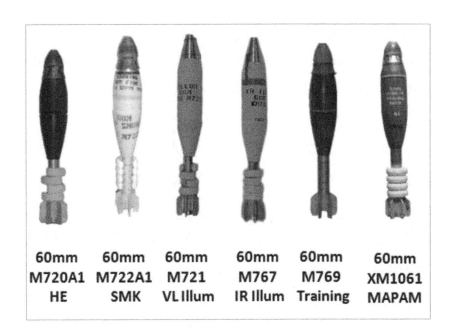

60mm M720A1 HE	60mm M722A1 SMK	60mm M721 VL Illum	60mm M767 IR Illum	60mm M769 Training	60mm XM1061 MAPAM

Characteristics of NVA and VC Mortars

Easily portable and simple to operate, the mortar was ideally suited to the terrain of South Vietnam and the tactics of the NVA and, in particular, the Viet Cong. Ever conscious of US firepower, a well-trained mortar team could set up a mortar position out of the sight of the enemy, fire off a number of rounds at maximum range and, due to the mortar rounds' long flight time, be moving away from the firing site before the first rounds impacted on the target. Such maneuverability severely restricted allied counter-mortar fire or retaliation by air.

The mortar was particularly suited for attacking standoff targets, such as US firebases or installations, where its greater accuracy over the rocket allowed it to be used against point targets.

The NVA and VC deployed a wide variety of mortars, ranging in size from the small 50mm to the breech-loaded 160mm. However, the most common types were the light Chicom Type 63 60mm mortar, Soviet M1937 and M1943 82mm mortars, and the Soviet M1938 and M1943 120mm mortars.

The enemy wasn't partial in their use of mortars. They used mortars and shells made by the Russians, Chinese, and some Eastern bloc countries.

NVA mortar positions were often cynically sited near inhabited areas so the crew could seek refuge from air attack after firing a few rounds. The mortar position itself was generally a hole approximately 1.7-meters deep and two meters in diameter, invariably excellently camouflaged, with only the mortar tube fire path uncovered during firing. These mortars were frequently sited to fire along the long axis of the target to take advantage of their small deflection error.

The lightweight 60mm mortar, weighing only forty-five pounds when assembled for firing, was an ideal standoff weapon. The crew could fire it, then pick it up, and move with it. With a maximum range of nearly two kilometers and a minimum range of only ninety meters, it also made for an excellent infantry support weapon.

VC mortar crew

Throughout the Vietnam War, US soldiers interacted with the nearby villagers in an attempt to win over their hearts and minds. Troops were trained in their native dialects and supplied them with much needed food and medical supplies. These locals were a valuable source of information regarding enemy troop strength and movement. Often these locals were even allowed on base to perform a number of various domestic services for the GIs (See Chapter 14).

However, since it was impossible to distinguish a "friendly" from a VC, all information was intensely scrutinized. And on more than a few occasions, those same "friendlies" allowed on base could be seen strolling and counting their steps to give the VC mortar crews more exact distances between the base perimeter and the bunkers that protected troops and munitions. Of course, as soon as observed, they were taken into custody and interrogated.

Viet Cong soldiers

Enemy Tactics

In a single instance of a mortar and recoilless rifle* attack conducted against an air base in Vietnam, a minimum of 240 rounds were fired by the Viet Cong from 81 and 82mm mortars and recoilless rifles. A plot of the rounds indicated that the aircraft parking areas and other operating installations adjacent to taxiways and runways were the primary targets. The Viet Cong attack was apparently well planned in detail and vigorously executed without any prior warning.

No incidents or patterns were evident which could have been considered as specific indicators of the attack and, militarily, the attack could be rated a complete success. The Viet Cong had obviously infiltrated the area often enough to reconnoiter and plan an attack that succeeded in damaging US aircraft and inflicting heavy personnel casualties. This represented just one of their many successful maneuvers.

Most Viet Cong mortar and recoilless rifle attacks lasted no longer than twenty minutes; however, they could cause considerable damage in a short period of time. The immediate detection of the firing positions was essential if they were to shorten the duration of the attack. Where possible, continuous aerial observation would be maintained during the hours of darkness, with particular interest paid from 2200 hours until one hour before the beginning of morning nautical twilight. This period was considered the most likely time of attack. The incidents highlighted in the following attacks clearly illustrate this requirement for continuous aerial observation:

- During an attack on Soc Trang, at 0150 hours on June 22, 1966 , a UH-1D helicopter and an O1-F fixed-wing aircraft were airborne. The O1-F aircraft pilot spotted the initial enemy firing and immediately dropped a flare above the spotted gun position. Before the flare had deployed and ignited, which took about forty seconds, seven more rounds had already landed. The attack lasted only five minutes but, without the immediate detection of the firing positions, additional rounds would have been fired resulting in increased damage and casualties.

- In a mortar attack on Vinh Long on June 7, 1966, the armed aircraft that had been acting as aerial observers for the base was refueling at the time of the raid. They immediately scrambled and brought direct fire on the VC positions. In this case, the defending elements took immediate action; however, the need for continuous surveillance was evident.

- A helicopter fire team on reconnaissance at the Vinh Long airfield spotted the first rounds as they were fired toward the base on May 29, 1966. The team passed the alert to the airfield tower and took the enemy positions under fire. An AC-47 flare ship was diverted from the nearby Can Tho area.

Tom Pisapia

The remaining armed ships on the air-field scrambled and fired on the positions within six minutes, at which time enemy action ceased.

The M40 recoilless rifle is a lightweight, portable, crew-served 105 mm recoilless rifle made in the United States. Intended primarily as an antitank weapon, it could also be employed in an antipersonnel role with the use of an antipersonnel tracer flechette rounds (See Chapter 17).

The US purposely gave ammo to the Communists in the Vietnam War.

There was no unconventional war like the one that played out behind the scenes of the greater war in Vietnam. One small aspect of that hidden war was Project Eldest Son, a plan that would take out the enemy's individual infantry rifles using its own ammunition.

It was carried out by a US military entity called the Studies and Observations Group, the Special Forces unit behind many of the top-secret missions and operations inside the Military Assistance Command Vietnam. The unit was in many of the major battles and offensives of the war, including the Tet Offensive and the Easter Offensive. But Project Eldest Son was different. It was a slow burn, a subtle influx of materiel into the enemy's supply and ammunition depots, with one marked difference—one that wouldn't show itself until it was too late.

Starting in 1967, the United States and

Tom Pisapia

the MACV-SOG began sending the communist forces throughout the area ammunition for the AK-47 machine guns and even mortars. They all looked ordinary, but they didn't work like any ordinary ammo—and they weren't just duds either. These rounds were filled with enough high explosives, not just to fire the projectiles but to destroy the weapon and severely wound the shooter. For the mortar rounds, the explosives, together, could kill an entire mortar crew.

After a while, the United States hoped the Vietnamese Communists would be afraid to use their own weapons and ammo. Killing the enemy was a good side effect, but the SOG needed some of them to survive.

For two years, special operators all over Vietnam would capture ammunition and supply centers, infuse cases of ammo with the faulty ammunition and then let it end up back in the hands of the enemy. Like everything in Vietnam, you never knew what might be boo-by-trapped. Eventually, the SOG would have to warn US troops against using communist weapons and ammo over the defective new M-16 to prevent the explosives from killing friendlies.

The program only ended because it was leaked to the media in the West, but even so, its efficacy was never fully known.

Tom Pisapia

CHAPTER 14

Hooch Maids and a Barber Too

A hooch maid was a South Vietnamese woman employed to clean the shelters and keep house for American servicemen during the Vietnam War.

These women typically worked six days a week, cleaning and maintaining the rooms and belongings of the soldiers. If their work quality was deemed to be satisfactory, they could be given goods from the base exchange, which were quickly turned into extra income on the black market. If they were paid in cash, it would usually range from eight to ten dollars per month per GI they supported. This wage would put them in the upper-end range of earners in their villages and was as much as a captain in the South Vietnamese Army earned.

The military generally allowed most officers and noncommissioned men to have hooch maids, whenever these men wanted and requested their services. In some of the bigger bases, military trucks picked up the maids at designated stops every morning and returned them in the evening. Issues often arose between the soldiers and the maids, due to cultural differences, including how to clean clothes properly and how much soap to use when washing the clothes. Maids also cooked for the men when appropriate.

Although their duties were usually limited to doing the wash, shining boots, or making the bunk, some maids reportedly had sex with soldiers to earn extra income. The GIs couldn't pick their hooch maids, rather a certain number of them were assigned to each hooch.

Unfortunately the hooch maids also brought with them sexually transmitted diseases including gonorrhea and syphilis. In addition, the unprotected sex resulted in a number of these hooch maids getting pregnant by their GI counterparts. They also were a steady source of drug delivery on many bases.

At FSB Buttons, they even had a barber who would make frequent visits to the base and gave a decent haircut—not much for frills since he set up a chair or two in the middle of the compound. No stale-dated magazines or even an old dog-eared copy of *Playboy* could be found in this makeshift place of business, but it got the job done.

The barber seemed friendly enough and could speak just enough broken English to make small talk. Most of the GIs found this service a great help since long hair sure didn't work well in the sweltering heat and humidity of everyday life in Vietnam.

"One month later, after the snake-bite incident, while guarding a small airstrip, a C-130 plane had just unloaded its usual 'beer and bullets' cargo and quickly took off again. It circled the fire base, landed and burned to the ground. The flames were so intense from the burning airplane fuel that a flyer's side arm actually melted from the heat. My first instinct was to pick up the weapon, but I knew that this would be an investigation site and it was better left alone.

"Intelligence said it was shot down by the barber that used to visit our base. He turned out to be VC. They found a .50-caliber machine gun pointed through the top of his hooch in his nearby village. Song Be Fire Base Buttons was one hundred miles north of Saigon and eighteen miles from the Ho Chi Minh Trail."

Tom Pisapia

AC-130A (FT) USAF taxiing Da Nang AB,
South Vietnam 1972 IP

Beginning in 1965, the C-130 Hercules—
with its four turbo-prop engines, superior
fifteen-ton payload, and its ability to rapidly
offload palletized cargo—dominated airlift
operations in Vietnam. As ground combat
increased, so did airlift requirements. The
C-130 aircraft and crews rotated into South
Vietnam every few weeks from bases in the
Philippines, Taiwan, Okinawa, and Japan.

Many tactical airlift missions were anything
but routine. Bad weather, mountainous or

jungle terrain, enemy action, the condition of forward airstrips, crowded air space, and ground space congested with helicopters, trucks, and people all contributed to eventful missions.

Airlift crew training in the US that was dependent on instrument flying proved inadequate for flight operations in Southeast Asia. Crews adapted quickly and learned to fly visually and under low ceilings when possible and to use their own wits and judgment. Despite these challenges and more, the cargo was almost always delivered.

CHAPTER 15

In-Country R&R

There were two in-country R&R destinations: Da Nang (China Beach) for the Marines and Vung Tau for the Army.

"While in Vietnam, the subject of R&R was brought up. The old guys would tell us to put in for it as soon as possible because of there being so many troops wanting to do the same thing. So that was what I made sure to take care of. We all were entitled to a three-day, in-country R&R and a seven-day out of country R&R.

"I got my three-day R&R when I left Song Be and was stationed at a duster compound further south. My three days would be spent in Vung Tau by the coast.

"The means of transportation was always by helicopter, truck, jeep—whatever they threw at you. It wasn't pretty. Once you arrived, you would flag down a ride, get a room, usually split with other GIs to share the cost of the rundown hotels you found. We spent a day at the beach and hung out at bars in the hotels at night, spinning our stories and shooting the bull. Even went to see the Buddhist temples for a little cultural tour.

"On the last night of R&R, we were celebrating probably a bit too hard and thought that we should treat ourselves to a rickshaw ride. We were enjoying the ride and not really paying any attention to where the driver was taking us. He dropped us off in what seemed to be a small nightlife district where we were immediately approached by Vietnamese police officers. They pulled their guns and I soon had a .45-caliber pistol pointed at my head, with one of them yelling at me 'You VC?' I guess that struck me pretty funny, being six foot three, 170 pounds of blond-haired Norwegian, so I said, 'Do we look like VC?'

"Well, that response did not sit well with the head cop and we were all thrown in a cell. As we spent the next few hours behind bars contemplating our fate, it seemed obvious that the police didn't have any intention of letting us go, so I concocted a scheme.

"I told the head guy that we had to be on a helicopter and back at the base by tomorrow or heads would roll. They acted dumb and were probably looking for a bribe, but they let us go immediately. The other GIs thought I did a great job calling their bluff and, once the smoke cleared and we were on our way, we laughed our asses off over it. Dumb GIs!

"It seems that the rickshaw driver dropped us off in an area of Vung Tau that was off-limits to GIs. Whether the police were looking out for us or just looking for a bribe, I'll never know. But the VC had been known to scour the less secure areas of Vung Tau, looking to slit the throats of GIs who had wandered off the beaten path.

"The three days there just seemed to fly by and then back to the duster compound and back to reality. There was a war going on and you were always on guard—trusted no one other than the GIs you were with."

But how did they pay for this kind of "luxurious" three-day R&R vacation? A Specialist E4 was paid $214.20 per month plus an extra fifty-five dollars for taking hostile fire and thirteen dollars per month for foreign duty. Of course, to earn this staggering wage of $282.20 per month, they were on duty 24–7!

However, the military was not handing out cash to the GIs on their monthly payday. They were given military payment certificates, or MPCs. These MPCs could be used in the PXs (Post Exchanges) and clubs on base, in lieu of the dollars, if they happened to be near one. But, as with most things, a black market evolved for these MPCs as well.

The locals in Vietnam wanted real US currency to deposit in their bank accounts. Dollars represented real value rather than their local currency, the piaster, which fluctuated with the wind and was devaluated by unpredictable and often rampant inflation.

The United States, while trying to help the local economy, set the official rate at about 125 piaster for one dollar MPC. However, a local could offer as much as three times the value in piasters to get a military MPC. But the MPCs were worthless to the locals since they could not redeem them anywhere. So, they would trade them to the GIs for US dollars, often offering two MPCs for one dollar. The GIs would have dollars sent from home and the locals would trade them two hundred dollars of MPCs for one hundred dollars in US currency! The GIs could then exchange the two hundred dollars of MPCs for a two hundred dollar money order and send it back home.

CHAPTER 16

Suicide

"It was mid-June 1968 and I was sent to a new location sixty miles outside of Saigon. I was finally able to work my MOS, which was radio and teletype. I had a secret clearance at this time working with S2* on troop movements. During this time, we had one of our troops get a 'Dear John letter' and he shot himself, putting the barrel of his M-16 under his chin while in the guard tower. The company was brought to attention while they lowered his body—a very sad day."

*S2 handles security clearances and provides information about the "battle-scape," to include weather, news

Tom Pisapia

reports, and anything pertinent to the mission.

According to the National Archives, during the Vietnam War, 382 GIs died of self-inflicted wounds, but this number is deceptive and does not reflect the estimated 150,000 to 200,000 Vietnam veterans who have committed suicide since returning home from the war.

The truth is that no one knows the true number. There are no reliable statistics about veteran suicides. Most states and localities do not submit suicide reports to the VA, and in many cases, the local examiners are not sure if the death was indeed self-inflicted. As a result, while we are confronted with overwhelming and heart-wrenching evidence indicating that suicide has become far more prevalent among veterans since the Vietnam War, the statistics that might clearly define the scope of the problem simply don't exist, and we are seeing only a fraction of the problem. Realistic numbers will never become available from the government or military because of the negative impact they would have on the costs of VA health care or on the recruiting efforts so vital to the all-volunteer military. Suicides among active-duty troops are also at record levels, killing more of our soldiers than enemy actions in recent years.

In 2012 alone, an estimated 7,500 former military personnel died by suicide. More active duty veterans, 177, succumbed to suicide that year than were killed in combat, 176. The Army suffered 52 percent of the suicides from all branches.

In 2013, the VA released a study that covered suicides from 1999 to 2010, which showed that roughly twenty-two veterans were dying by suicide per day, or one every sixty-five minutes. Some sources suggest that this rate may be undercounting suicides. A recent analysis found a suicide rate among veterans of about thirty per one hundred thousand population per year, compared with the civilian rate of fourteen per one hundred thousand. However, the comparison was not adjusted for age and sex.

The total number of suicides differs by age group; 31 percent of these suicides were by veterans forty-nine and younger while 69 percent were by veterans age fifty and older.

Truthfully, PTSD is not a "disorder." Post-traumatic stress "damage" is a normal and predictable reaction to the horrors of war, the heart and soul's reaction to the unthinkable destruction of brick and mortar and life and limb.

For years, the Department of Veterans Affairs reported an average of twenty veterans dying by suicide every day—an often-cited statistic that raised alarm nationwide about the rate of veteran suicide.

The VA has now revealed that the average daily number of veteran suicides has always included the deaths of active-duty service members and members of the National Guard and Reserve, not just veterans.

The VA released the National Suicide Data Report in 2018, which included data from 2005 through 2015. Much in the report remained unchanged from two years prior, when the VA reported suicide statistics through 2014. Veteran suicide rates are still higher than the rest of the population, particularly among women.

In both reports, the VA said an average of twenty veterans succumbed to suicide every day. In its newest version, the VA was more specific.

The report shows the total is 20.6 suicides every day. Of those, 16.8 were veterans and 3.8 were active-duty service members, guards-men, and reservists, according to the report. That amounts to 6,132 veterans and 1,387 service members who died by suicide in one year.

VA officials determine the statistic by analyzing state death certificates and calculating the percentage of veterans out of all suicides. The death certificates include a field designating whether the deceased ever served in the US military.

Information in the 2012 report wasn't as complete as the newer ones. At the time, only twenty-one states shared information from their death certificates. California and Texas, which have large veteran populations, were two of the states that did not provide their data.

Tom Pisapia

The report shows that of the 20.6 veterans and service members who died by suicide every day, six had recently used VA health care services. The suicide rate among the people who did not receive VA care increased faster than the ones who did.

In May 2019, President Donald Trump signed an executive order called the PREVENTS Initiative to counter the national tragedy of suicide. The initiative aims to equip state and local governments with the resources necessary to identify and intervene in scenarios where US veterans may be at risk to suicide. In the past, the VA and other federal agencies relied upon the veteran to self-identify when needing help. The new initiative attempts to bring public awareness of the veterans' struggle associated with service. The president successfully secured a record $73.1 billion dollars for veteran health services. Included in the funding is $8.6 billion toward mental health services.

The 2018 federal budget expanded mental health screenings for veterans.

CHAPTER 17

Out-of-Country R&R

Beehives

Tom Pisapia

"With forty-five days left in country, I took my seven-day, out-of-country R&R to Australia, the land Down Under. We flew into Sydney, hailed a taxi, rented a room, and we were off checking the sights. We visited the famous Sydney Opera House, which was amazing to see. I do remember that it was tiring on my legs with all the steps leading up to the place. My friends and I spent a lot of time at the beach and as you probably know it wasn't all swimming. After the swim we'd head back to the room, freshen up, grab a bite to eat, and hit the pubs.

"In Australia at that time, they used to have men pubs and women pubs that they would go to after work, but later at night they would meet up at the clubs. I do remember Kings Cross, which was an area that was crowded with nightclubs. I was amazed by one of the clubs that had different music on every floor, rock 'n' roll on the ground floor, country on the second floor, and ballroom dancing on the third floor. I think it was called the Checker Club, but it's been so long I'm not sure. What a gas!

"We took a night and went to the famous revolving tower restaurant in Sydney. It was pricey but what a meal. It had been a long time since I had a steak—what a treat!

"What a lot of people don't realize is that when you flush the toilet Down Under, it turns in the opposite direction. We got a good chuckle out of that, but I guess when you're young, you laugh at the little things. Laughs were too few and at a premium and we appreciated every one of them.

"But as we know, all good things must come to an end and then back to reality. We headed back to the crap with no money left. I do remember that I took seven hundred dollars with me on the trip, so one hundred a day went for a great time.

"The Aussies were great people and I was very proud to have known them. They were great allies in Vietnam too. They took part in many major battles in Vietnam and I'm not sure that they got all the respect that was due to them. Thank you to my Aussie friends."

Tom Pisapia

After South Korea and Thailand, Australia provided the most extensive military support to the United States in Vietnam. Their commitment of almost sixty thousand personnel was dominated by the Army, which included the elite SAS, but also featured Air Force and Navy elements. Their most decorated unit of the war was the Australian Army Training Team Vietnam (AATTV), whose advisers worked with US Special Forces between 1962 and 1972 to train ARVN (Army of the Republic of Vietnam) and indigenous troops.

Battle of Coral/Balmoral

Australian, New Zealand, and US forces were involved in a series of actions between May and June 1968 at Fire Support Bases Coral and Balmoral some twenty kilometers north of Bien Hoa city. Sitting astride a route used by North Vietnamese and Viet Cong forces approaching or departing Saigon and nearby Bien Hoa, the bases comprised defended positions for artillery, mortars, and armored vehicles that, in turn, supported infantry patrols of the area.

The North Vietnamese launched several strong attacks in an attempt to drive the Australians from this important area. The Australians also initiated combat during their many patrols outside the bases. These actions, over a twenty-five day period, made up Australia's costliest and most protracted battle of the Vietnam War.

Coral attack one

Early on the morning of May 13, 1968, just hours after Australian and New Zealand forces had established Fire Support Base Coral, North Vietnamese troops attacked in strength. The Australian rifle companies had taken up ambush positions up to four kilometers from Coral, inside the perimeter were a collection of units or parts thereof, including 102nd Field Battery and the 1st Battalion, Royal Australian Regiment's (1RAR) mortar platoon.

A series of unforeseen circumstances led to delays in setting up the base on May 12, and the flurry of activity in the area, as helicopters carrying men and equipment came and went, was watched by North Vietnamese observers.

On the first night of its existence, Coral was vulnerable. When the North Vietnamese assault came 102nd Battery's artillery, its machine gunners and the mortar platoon were directly in the enemy's path. Fighting raged around their positions, with the mortar men in danger of being overrun. The machine gunners, out in front of the artillery and having already suffered casualties, were forced to brave intense fire and run for the relative safety of the gun positions. But these also fell under heavy attack.

For the first time since the Second World War, Australian artillerymen were fighting in close defense of their guns, one of which was overrun before being recaptured.

Threatened with annihilation, the mortar platoon's commanding lieutenant called for splintex* to be fired on his own position. The mortar men pressed themselves against the earth while five rounds of the flesh-tearing steel darts, of which splintex shells consisted, swept over their heads, tearing enemy soldiers apart and leaving only dead men around the Australian position.

Splintex was the Australian term for what Americans called flechettes or beehives.

The Australians were fortunate that night. In addition to the composure of the officers and men who faced the attack, the weight of defensive fire—from the 102nd Battery, from a New Zealand battery more than a kilometer away, from helicopters, and from aircraft—was too great for the North Vietnamese to withstand.

The Australian survivors were shaken by the experience; first light revealed fifty-two enemy bodies while drag marks leading into the scrub suggested that many more dead men had been removed from the battlefield. On the Australian side, nine soldiers had lost their lives and an additional twenty-eight were wounded.

The Australians participation in the Vietnam War resulted in 521 casualties and over three thousand wounded. A total of 15,381 conscripted national servicemen served from 1965 to 1972, sustaining 202 killed and 1,279 wounded.

A beehive was an antipersonnel round packed with metal flechettes fired from an artillery gun usually deployed during ground conflict. It is also known as flechette rounds or their official designation, antipersonnel-tracer (APERS-T).

The flechette rounds were developed under a contract administered by Picatinny Arsenal and awarded to the Whirlpool Corporation in April 1957. The contract was named the "Beehive Program," referring to the way the flechettes were compartmentalized and stacked, looking like the traditional image of a conical beehive.

The first example was the 105mm howitzer M546 anti personnel tracer (APERS-T), first fired in combat in 1966 and thereafter used extensively in the Vietnam War. Intended for direct fire against enemy troops, the M546 was direct-fired from a near horizontally leveled 105 mm howitzer and ejected eight thousand flechettes during flight by a mechanical time fuse. Green starshells were shot into the air prior to their use to warn friendly troops that such a round was about to be discharged.

The flechette shell is an antipersonnel weapon generally fired from a tank. The shell explodes in the air and releases thousands of metal darts 37.5 mm in length, which disperse in a conical arch three hundred meters long and about ninety meters wide.

The primary military advantage of the flechette over other munitions is its ability to penetrate dense vegetation very rapidly and to strike a relatively large number of enemy soldiers.

Soldiers reported that after beehive rounds were fired during an overrun attack, many enemy dead had their hands nailed to the wooden stocks of their rifles and these dead could be dragged to mass graves by their rifle.

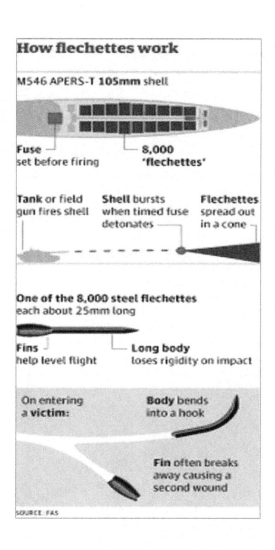

How flechettes work

M546 APERS-T **105mm** shell

Fuse
set before firing

8,000
'flechettes'

Tank or field
gun fires shell

Shell bursts
when timed fuse
detonates

Flechettes
spread out
in a cone

One of the 8,000 steel flechettes
each about 25mm long

Fins
help level flight

Long body
loses rigidity on impact

On entering
a **victim:**

Body bends
into a hook

Fin often breaks
away causing a
second wound

SOURCE: FAS

Flashbacks 177

Tom Pisapia

CHAPTER 18

Letters, Food, and Salutes

"During our tour in Vietnam, probably the most important thing to all of us was letters and care packages from home. We would all gather around and wait for our names to be called. Hopefully, your name came up. We would all take time out to read about what was going on in the 'real world,' as we called it, sitting on the ground, sandbags, or whatever was convenient. Letters first and then we would dive into those care packages for the good stuff.

"Chocolate cookies were a favorite packed in popcorn so they wouldn't get broken; Kool-

Aid to put in our drinking water that always tasted like crap; maybe a can of spam that we would heat up with a chunk of C-4* out of a claymore mine to make a sandwich. This didn't happen that often but we thought it was a great treat. Sitting around talking to each other about what we hoped to do when we returned home, if we were able to get out of that hellhole. We were from all parts of the USA and, no matter who you talked to, we all seemed to have the same thoughts. Most of the time, you received mail during down time or when you were in a more secured area."

*C-4 or Composition C-4 is a common variety of the plastic explosive family known as Composition C. It has a texture like modeling clay and can be molded into any desired shape. C-4 can be exploded only by the shock wave from a detonator or blasting cap.

If ignited, the C-4 would burn and not explode. Lighting it with a match just made it burn slowly, like a piece of wood.

Of course, we couldn't do that at night, because we might attract the attention of the enemy, so most of the time our meals were eaten cold.

There is much confusion regarding the combat food rations that were supplied to our GIs. Below is a brief history of how US military meals evolved.

The K-ration was an individual daily combat food ration introduced by the US Army during World War II. Originally intended as an individually packaged daily ration for issue to airborne troops, tank crews, motorcycle couriers, and other mobile forces for short durations. The K-ration provided three separately boxed meal units: breakfast, supper, and dinner. The final version totaled 2,830 calories. The first procurement of K-rations was made in May 1942.

The meals only gained "palatable" and "better than nothing" ratings from the soldiers.

During the China Burma India Theater of operations during WW II, many soldiers, including the US unit known as Merrill's Marauders and the British Chindit forces in Burma, had lived primarily on K-rations for five months, supplemented by rice, tea, sugar, jam, bread, and canned meat rations dropped to them by air. In the case of the Marauders, whose diet consisted of 80 percent K-rations, severe weight loss (an average of 35 pounds per man) and vitamin deficiency were noted.

Two British special ops soldiers from the elite Chindit squad, some months after they had last eaten K-rations, were on their base when it was visited by quartermaster logistics officers. Upon seeing the visitors carrying K-rations, both seasoned special ops soldiers vomited.

In 1948, after introduction of improvements in the C-ration, the K-ration was declared obsolete.

The C-ration was a prepared and canned wet combat ration intended to be issued to US military land forces when fresh food (A-ration) or packaged unprepared food (B-ration) prepared in mess halls or field kitchens was not possible or available and when a survival ration (K-ration or D-ration*) was insufficient. Development began in 1938 with the first rations being field-tested in 1940 and wide-scale adoption following soon after.

D-ration bar was created to meet four objectives:

1. Weigh 4 ounces

2. Be high in food energy value

3. Be able to withstand high temperatures

4. Taste "a little better than a boiled potato" (to keep soldiers from eating their emergency rations in nonemergency situations)

The D ration was almost universally detested for its bitter taste by US troops and was often discarded instead of consumed when issued. Troops called the D-ration "Hitler's Secret Weapon" for its effect on soldiers' " intestinal tracts.

The C-ration was replaced in 1958 with the meal combat individual (MCI).

Although officially a new ration, the MCI was derived from and very similar to the original C-Ration, and in fact continued to be called "C-Rations" by American troops throughout its production life as a combat ration (1958–1980).

Although the replacement for the MCI, the MRE (meals ready to eat), was formally adopted as the Department of Defense combat ration in 1975, the first large-scale production test did not occur until in 1978 with the first MRE I rations packed and delivered in 1981. While the MRE officially replaced the MCI in 1981, previously packed MCI rations continued to be issued until depleted.

While MREs should be kept cool, they do not need to be refrigerated. They have also been distributed to civilians during natural disasters.

Some of the early MRE main courses were not very palatable, earning them the nicknames "meals rejected by everyone," "meals rarely edible," and even "meals rejected by Ethiopians" (in reference to the 1983–85 famine in Ethiopia).

Some of the individual portions even had their own nicknames. For example, the frankfurters, which came sealed in pouches of four, were referred to as "the four fingers of death."

Although quality has improved over the years, many of the nicknames have stuck. MREs were sometimes called "three lies for the price of one;" "it's not a meal, it's not ready;" and "you can't eat it."

Their low dietary fiber content could cause constipation in some, so they were also known as "meals requiring enemas,", "meals refusing to exit," "meals refusing to excrete," or "massive rectal expulsions."

While the myth that the gum found in MREs contains a laxative is false (however, they are sweetened with xylitol, a mild laxative), the crackers in the ration pack do contain a higher than normal vegetable content to facilitate digestion.

A superstition exists among troops about the Charms candies that come with some menus: they are considered bad luck, especially if they were actually eaten.

Early in the war in Afghanistan, among the international troops who mingled at Bagram Air Base, a single French 24-hour (three meal) combat ration (cassoulet, perhaps, with deer pâté and nougat) could be traded for at least five American MREs.

The vegetable cheese omelet MRE, Recipe No. 4, introduced in 2005, is generally considered the worst ever. Soldiers serving in Iraq dubbed it the "vomelet," both for its appearance and taste. It was discontinued in 2009.

Each MCI weighed approximately 2.7 pounds and contained about 1,200 calories.

Most recently, MREs have been developed using the Dietary Reference Intake, created by the Institute of Medicine (IOM). The IOM indicated service members (who were classified as highly active men between the ages of eighteen and thirty) typically burn about four thousand two hundred calories a day. However even if a GI were to consume three MREs per day, he would still suffer an negative energy balance.

In conclusion, throughout our military history, we have underfed our GIs, not even giving them enough nourishment to sustain them in the field. We have given them food that tasted so bad that they would rather throw it away and go hungry. Whether they called them K, C, MCI, or MRE, it was all S H I T!

A selection of United States military C-ration cans from World War II with items displayed. Note that the Old Gold cigarettes and vanilla caramels were not part of the C ration.

Elements of a United States military meal combat individual (MCI) ration, as served in Da Nang, South Vietnam during the Vietnam War, 1966 or 1967. It is still commonly referred to as "C-rations."

"After returning from the field and stationed at the net control station at the duster compound, a friend of mine and I hopped a jeep to the PX to spend some cash on a few things. After that we thought it would be nice to go and have a refreshment at the base bar and listen to some entertainment. The entertainment was a bunch of Vietnamese trying to play American music, but you took what you could get. Hah! On the way, walking down the sidewalk, we came upon a captain walking toward us. As he reached us, I had my right hand full, so being caught off guard, I saluted with my left hand and kept walking. In the back of my mind, I thought, 'What did I just do?' Well, it didn't take long, maybe four or five steps, and I heard, 'Troop, come here.' I walked over to the officer and said, "'Yes, sir?' He said, 'Do you know that you are supposed to salute an officer when approached?' With a lump in my throat, I managed to blurt out, 'I apologize, sir. I have been in the field and hadn't done that for a while.' He looked down at my boots and looked back at me and said, 'I see that' as he shook my hand. He then said, 'Be on your way, soldier,' with a faint smile, 'and don't forget to respect your commanders.'

"Well, we got to the bar and my friend said to me, 'You need to show a little more respect toward your commanders!' Needless to say, we both just lost it in laughter. Then my buddy wanted to give me lessons on how to salute. Crazy GIs."

Tom Pisapia

CHAPTER 19

Distraught GI and Duster Compound

"A few months had passed, and I had thirty-five days left in country. I was in the radio shack when I heard an M-16 rifle go off. I ran over to see what had happened and found three soldiers shot, one in the neck and one in the leg and one in the hip. I was the first one there, so I helped them get out of their chairs and on to the floor, until more help came. We found out later that it was a soldier that just could not take it anymore. This was a Duster compound*—more rats, snakes, bugs, and 115-degree heat."

*Duster compound

Starting in the fall of 1966, the US Army deployed three battalions of Dusters to the Republic of Vietnam, each battalion consisting of a headquarters battery and four Duster batteries, and each augmented by one attached Quad-50 battery and an artillery searchlight battery.

Despite a few early air kills, the air threat posed by North Vietnam never materialized and ADA crews found themselves increasingly involved in ground support missions. Most often the M42 tank was on point security, convoy escort, or perimeter defense. The Duster, as it was called by US troops in Vietnam, was soon found to excel in ground support. The 40mm guns proved to be effective against massed infantry attacks.

A total of three thousand seven hundred M42s were built. The vehicle has a crew of six and weighed 49,500 pounds, fully loaded. Maximum speed was forty-five mph with a range of one hundred miles. Armament con-

Tom Pisapia

sists of fully automatic twin 40mm M2A1 Bofors, (an anti-aircraft autocannon), with a rate of fire of 2×120 rounds per minute (rpm) and either a .30 caliber Browning M1919A4 or 7.62mm M60 machine gun.

A Duster M42 Tank at Song Be FSB Buttons

CHAPTER 20

Coming Home

January 31, 1969

"With only fifty days left in country, we were considered short-timers. So, you didn't take many risks leaving the base compound. You would walk around, and someone would say 'hi' and you would say 'short.' Then you would tell them how many days you had left, with a smile and a thumbs-up. It seemed like that fifty days took forever. Finally, the time had arrived.

"A jeep gave us a ride to the processing area where you were back standing in lines again. We always said it was hurry up and wait—the army way of doing things. Stand in line while they went through your whole baggage, which was the stuff you were taking home with you. While I was in line, a troop a couple places ahead of me was having his stuff gone through when I saw a frown on the inspector's face. He had reached into the troop's duffel bag and found a bottle of Johnson's talcum powder.

"He held it up and cut the bottom off of it and there was a bag of pot. We all looked at each other and shook our heads and thought 'Dumb; ain't he dumb.' Powder on the top and pot on the bottom. How the inspector knew it was there made us scratch our heads. Needless to say, the troop was taken away by the military police. I'm sure it wasn't the first time the inspector had run across this problem. So, instead of going home, this poor GI was going to do some time.

"Time to board the plane for home. We all get in our seats and the captain said, 'Fasten your seat belts, soldiers; we are headed for the USA.' As you can probably imagine, there was a lot of talking going on, but when he said that, the roar of the engines had already begun. The cheers were so deafening that you couldn't hear the engines and there was a tear in all our eyes and a chill ran up and down our spines.

"The flight home was shorter than the trip there, because we flew up over Alaska and then to Oakland, California. Arriving in Oakland, we could not wait to get out of uniform due to the Vietnam demonstrators calling us baby killers and calling out vulgar language at us. However, we held our heads high, because we had been through a lot more shit than they could give us.

"Flew into Chicago. It was five below zero and a foot of snow on the ground. I was one of the lucky ones that had a family there to meet me. There where kisses and hugs and American food.

"It took me about a year to get used to the weather back home after being in that hellhole. Now it was time for me to enter the next chapter of my life. All my thanks and love go out to all my comrades that I served with. May God bless you all."

Tom Pisapia

Many things had been going on in the States over the last one year, one month and ten days while Dean was in country. He certainly didn't have access to a daily newspaper or any source of news to keep him updated on the events unfolding back home. He might have seen an occasional copy of *Stars and Stripes* when he was back at the Fire Base. Although I have the utmost respect for S&S, it had to sugarcoat the war news a bit. We already had a major troop morale issue and it certainly did not want to make it any worse.

Although Dean had experienced the Tet Offensive firsthand during the first half of 1968, he had no idea what the effect of that massive North Vietnamese offensive had on the attitude of the American public toward the war in Vietnam.

The launch of the Tet Offensive by North Vietnamese communist troops in January 1968 and its early successes against US and South Vietnamese troops sent waves of shock and discontent across the home front and sparked the most intense period of antiwar protests to date. The ability of the NVA to conduct such a coordinated and far-reaching offensive clearly proved that the war's end was nowhere in sight. In addition, General West-moreland's claim that he would need to call up the reserves and send two hundred thousand more troops to Vietnam clearly showed that the newspaper accounts of our successes in Vietnam were grossly exaggerated.

By early February 1968, a Gallup Poll showed only 35 percent of the population approved of President Lyndon Johnson's han-dling of the war and a full 50 percent disap-proved (the rest had no opinion). Joining the antiwar demonstrations by this time were members of the organization Vietnam Vet-erans Against the War, many of whom were in wheelchairs and on crutches. The sight of these men on television throwing away the medals they had won during the war did much to win people over to the antiwar cause.

The antiwar movement had actually begun years before, but it was viewed as a fringe protest by small groups of peace activists and leftist intellectuals on college campuses. However, it gained national prominence in 1965 after the United States began bombing North Vietnam in earnest. Critics of the war had begun to question the government's assertion that it was fighting a democratic war to liberate the South Vietnamese people from communist aggression.

Antiwar marches and other protests, such as the ones organized by Students for a Democratic Society, attracted a widening base of support over the next three years, peaking in early 1968 after the successful Tet Offensive noted above.

Though the vast majority of the American population still supported the administration policy in Vietnam, a small but outspoken liberal minority was making its voice heard by the end of 1965. This minority included many students as well as prominent artists and intellectuals and members of the hippie movement, a growing number of young people who rejected authority and embraced the drug culture.

By November 1967, American troop strength in Vietnam was approaching five hundred thousand and US casualties had reached 15,058 killed and 109,527 wounded. The Vietnam War was costing the US some $25 billion per year, and disillusionment was beginning to reach greater sections of the taxpaying public. More casualties were reported in Vietnam every day, even as US commanders demanded more troops. Under the draft system, as many as forty thousand young men were called into service each month, adding fuel to the fire of the antiwar movement.

On October 21, 1967, one of the most prominent antiwar demonstrations took place, as some one hundred thousand protesters gathered at the Lincoln Memorial; around thirty thousand of them continued in a march on the Pentagon later that night. After a brutal confrontation with the soldiers and US marshals protecting the building, hundreds of demonstrators were arrested.

One of them was the author Norman Mailer, who chronicled the events in his book *The*

Armies of the Night, published the following year to widespread acclaim. Also in 1967, the antiwar movement got a big boost when the civil rights leader Martin Luther King Jr. went public with his opposition to the war on moral grounds, condemning the war's diversion of federal funds from domestic programs as well as the disproportionate number of African-American casualties in relation to the total number of soldiers killed in the war.

At 6:05 p.m. on Thursday, April 4, 1968, King was shot dead while standing on a balcony outside his second-floor room at the Lorraine Motel in Memphis, Tennessee. News of King's assassination prompted major outbreaks of racial violence, resulting in more than forty deaths nationwide and extensive property damage in over one hundred American cities.

Two months after the King assassination, on June 5, the hope of the antiwar movement, presidential candidate Robert F. Kennedy was shot after celebrating his victory in the California primary. He died the next morning.

Both Kennedy and Senator Eugene McCarthy of Minnesota had been running for the Democratic nomination at the time.

After many New Hampshire primary voters rallied behind the antiwar McCarthy, Johnson announced that he would not seek reelection. Vice President Hubert Humphrey ultimately accepted the Democratic nomination in August in Chicago, but a large number of antiwar demonstrators showed up outside the convention building.

Protesters descended on Chicago, bent on disrupting the convention. Chicago's Mayor Richard Daley, who had responded to riots in Chicago following King's assassination by giving police the order to "shoot to kill any arsonists or anyone with a Molotov cocktail," called up twelve thousand police officers. Backing them up were nearly six thousand Illinois National Guard and five thousand Army soldiers.

On Aug. 28, 1968, the streets of Chicago exploded into violence. Around ten thousand protesters gathered in Grant Park for the demonstration. At approximately 3:30

p.m., a young man lowered the American flag that was there. The police broke through the crowd and began beating the young man, while the crowd pelted the police with food, rocks, and chunks of concrete. The chants of some of the protesters shifted from "hell no, we won't go" to "pigs are whores."

Tom Hayden, one of the leaders of Students for a Democratic Society, encouraged protesters to move out of the park to ensure that if the police used tear gas on them, it would have to be done throughout the city. The amount of tear gas used to suppress the protesters was so great that it made its way to the Conrad Hilton Hotel, where it disturbed Hubert Humphrey while in his shower.

The police sprayed demonstrators and bystanders with mace and were taunted by some protesters with chants of "kill, kill, kill." The police assault in front of the Conrad Hilton Hotel on the evening of August 28 became the most famous image of the Chicago demonstrations of 1968. The entire event took place live under television lights for seventeen minutes with the crowd chanting, "The whole world is watching."

Police officers, exhausted and at the end of their rope, did not hold back. They pounded into the protesters with clubs and tear gas, striking indiscriminately and pressing the crowd back into Grant Park. At the back of the park, hundreds were pushed up against a plate glass window of the Hilton Hotel. It shattered, allowing an outlet for those being crushed and adding shards of broken glass to the bloody mix.

Antiwar protesters, defiant and bloodied, poured onto Michigan Avenue, determined to reach the International Amphitheater, where the Democratic National Convention continued into its third day.

Police lined the streets with sticks, shields, helmets, and tear gas. National Guardsmen, with heavy vehicles draped in razor wire, waited in reserve.

With growing frequency, the National Guard was called in to replace exhausted city cops who grew increasingly violent.

Tom Pisapia

In a telephone call to President Johnson on Saturday, September 7, 1968, Chicago Mayor Richard Daley described some of the activity undertaken by the elements of the protesters, whom he called "professional troublemakers." These activities included the burning of the American flag, raising of the Viet Cong flag, and throwing both manure and urine at the police.

Humphrey lost the 1968 presidential election to Richard M. Nixon, who promised in his campaign to restore "law and order"—a reference to conflict over antiwar protests as well as the rioting that followed King's assassination.

The following year, Nixon claimed, in a famous speech, that antiwar protesters constituted a small—albeit vocal—minority that should not be allowed to drown out the "silent majority" of Americans. Nixon's war policies divided the nation still further, however. In December 1969, the government instituted the first US draft lottery since World War II, inciting a vast amount of controversy and causing many young men to flee to Canada to avoid conscription. Tensions ran higher than ever, spurred on by mass demonstrations and incidents of official violence such as those at Kent State in May 1970, when National Guard troops shot into a group of protesters demonstrating against the US invasion of Cambodia, killing four students.

Perhaps if Dean had known more about the turmoil back in the States, it may have prepared him better for the bitter reception that he and his fellow GIs received on their return from the war. But, perhaps not.

CHAPTER 21

The Vietnam Veterans' Unique Story

The Vietnam War and the 2,709,918 soldiers who saw service in Vietnam, a number that represented 9.7% of their entire generation, presented our country with post-war challenges that differed from any previous wars.

I have identified six areas that made the Vietnam veterans much different than any other war veterans in US history and made their experience much more traumatic than those of previous warriors:

1. **Air travel made it possible for Vietnam GIs to enter the battlefield within forty-eight hours after leaving American soil and to return to society just as quickly.**

Even the forty thousand soldiers provided by the draft each month could not meet the insatiable demand for fresh troops in Vietnam. Within forty-eight hours of completing AIT, most troops set their feet on Vietnam soil. Also, the military's troop rotation policy of twelve to thirteen months in country made for constant turnover and retraining, often based on current needs rather than their military occupational specialty. The result was the inefficient and perpetual rotation of personnel. More experienced troops constantly being replaced by new and unseasoned personnel resulted in increased combat casualties and injuries and played a major role in their historically dismal troop morale.

Perhaps the slow-moving troop ships crossing either the Pacific or Atlantic during previous wars at least gave those returning veterans some time to decompress and interact with other GIs with whom they had served before they set foot on American soil. Actually, returning WWII veterans had a longer time before their return to the United States. It had taken four years to assemble the estimated 7.6 million troops overseas during WWII and four to six months to get them all home. And even then, they were forced to travel by train or bus to their ultimate destination.

The troop rotation policy was far different in WWII as well. Soldiers were deployed for the entire war and could be in active service for four to five years.

Similarly, it was not until a year after the armistice ending the Korean War that the remaining American divisions were withdrawn from Korea.

2. **Never had a nation used a defoliant to clear jungle growth and eliminate the enemy's food source without regard for the effect on its own troops.**

The spraying of twenty million gallons of an untested defoliant on the enemy, the jungle, and our own troops is thought to be linked to a dozen debilitating diseases. More details on Agent Orange use and effects are discussed in Chapter 11.

3. Never had returning troops been as disrespected upon their return to the States as those from Vietnam.

The contrast could not be greater between the greeting that WWII veterans received upon their return from war and the one that returning Vietnam veterans encountered. WW II was a clear-cut fight between good and evil. The unprovoked aggression of the armies of the Japanese and Germans were pitted against a united world coalition of nations to defeat them.

Even in the Korean War, although less clear-cut, an armistice ended the fighting and gave the returning veterans a welcome home for a job well done and at least a more positive view by the American people.

The Vietnam veteran received no such welcome and was derided in the press and in person after years of antiwar protests throughout the country had shifted its focus from antiwar to anti-veteran.

*Classic WWII welcome home
picture in Times Square*

Times Square Image Credit: Lt. Victor Jorgensen/US Navy/The LIFE Picture Collection via Getty Image

Sights that greeted the returning Vietnam veterans

Tom Pisapia

Moratorium to End The War image
Image credit: Charles H. Phillips/The LIFE
Picture Collection via Getty Images

4. Never had returning troops been shunned by their fellow veterans, who viewed them as having lost a war.

As returning Vietnam veterans sought some refuge among their fellow veterans at VFW, American Legion, and other veterans' organizations, they were shunned as having lost their war.

5. No recognition of the Vietnam combat trauma was even acknowledged until well after 1980 when the psych community finally announced its conclusions identifying PTSD as a condition.

Post-traumatic stress disorder first became the diagnosis we know today in 1980, when it was included in the Anxiety Disorders section of the Diagnostic and Statistical Manual of Mental Disorders-III (DSM-III) psychiatric manual. The DSM is the handbook used by health-care professionals in the United States and much of the world as the authoritative guide containing descriptions, symptoms, and other criteria for diagnosing mental disorders.

Before 1980, post-traumatic stress was described and diagnosed under a variety of different names. Throughout history, a variety of war-related references appear, such as battle fatigue, combat exhaustion, and shellshock. An acknowledgment existed that soldiers were affected by their war experience, but the trauma was more anecdotally referenced rather than in terms of an actual mental disorder. Without this identification, research and treatment was, of course, impossible.

6. **The inadequate, underfunded, and in many cases, incompetent VA system made these veterans even more reluctant to use their services.**

The VA has had a checkered past dating back to the Revolutionary War. Here are just a few of their most notable events:

1930—The Veterans Administration is established to replace the troubled Veterans Bureau that was plagued by corruption and scandal since its creation in 1921.

1945—President Harry Truman accepts the resignation of VA Administrator Frank Hines after a series of news reports detailing shoddy care in VA-run hospitals.

1946—The American Legion leads the charge seeking the ouster of VA Administrator

Gen. Omar Bradley, citing an ongoing lack of facilities, troubles faced by hundreds of thousands of veterans in getting services, and a proposal to limit access to services for some combat veterans.

1947—A government commission on reforming government uncovers enormous waste, duplication, and inadequate care in the VA system and calls for wholesale changes in the agency's structure.

1955—A second government reform commission again finds widespread instances of waste and poor care in the VA system, according to the Independent Institute.

1970s—Veterans grow increasingly frustrated with the VA for failing to better fund treatment and assistance programs and, later, to recognize exposure to the herbicide Agent Orange by troops in Vietnam as the cause for numerous medical problems among veterans.

1974—Vietnam veteran Ron Kovic, the subject of the book and movie, *Born on* *the Fourth of July*, leads a nineteen-day hunger strike at a federal building in Los Angeles to protest poor treatment of veterans in VA hospitals, demanding to meet with VA Director Donald Johnson. The ensuing uproar results in widespread criticism of Johnson. A few weeks later, Johnson resigns after President Richard Nixon announces an investigation into VA operations.

1976—A General Accounting Office investigation into Denver's VA hospital finds numerous shortcomings in patient care, including veterans whose surgical dressings are rarely changed. The GAO also looked at the New Orleans VA hospital and found ever-increasing patient loads were contributing to a decline in the quality of care there as well.

1981—Veterans camp out in front of the Wadsworth Veterans Medical Center in Los Angeles after the suicide of a former Marine who had rammed the hospital's lobby with his Jeep and fired shots into the wall after claiming the VA had failed to attend to his service-related disabilities.

1982—Controversial VA Director Robert Nimmo, who once described symptoms of exposure to the herbicide Agent Orange during the Vietnam War as little more than "teenage acne," resigns under pressure from veterans' groups.

The same year, the agency issues a report supporting veterans' claims that the VA had failed to provide them with enough information and assistance about Agent Orange exposure.

1984—Congressional investigators find evidence that VA officials had diverted or refused to spend more than $40 million that Congress approved to help Vietnam veterans with readjustment problems.

1986—The VA's Inspector General's office finds ninety-three physicians working for the agency have sanctions against their medical licenses, including suspensions and revocations, according to a 1988 GAO report.

1991—The *Chicago Tribune* reports that doctors at the VA's North Chicago hospital sometimes ignored test results, failed to treat patients in a timely manner, and conducted unnecessary surgery. The agency later takes responsibility for the deaths of eight patients, leading to the suspension of most surgery at the center.

1993—VA Deputy Undersecretary of Benefits R.J. Vogel testifies to Congress that a growing backlog of appeals from veterans denied benefits is due to a federal court established in 1988 to oversee the claims process. The VA, Vogel tells the lawmakers, is "reeling under this judicial review thing."

1999—Lawmakers open an investigation into widespread problems with clinical research procedures at the VA West Los Angeles Healthcare Center. The investigation followed years of problems at the hospital, including ethical violations by hospital researchers that included failing to get consent from some patients before conducting research involving them.

2000—The GAO finds "substantial problems" with the VA's handling of research trials involving human subjects.

2001—Despite a 1995 goal to reduce waiting times for primary care and specialty appointments to less than thirty days, the GAO finds that veterans still often wait more than two months for appointments.

2003—A commission appointed by President George W. Bush reports that as of January 2003, some 236,000 veterans had been waiting six months or more for initial or follow-up visits, "a clear indication," the commission said, "of lack of sufficient capacity or, at a minimum, a lack of adequate resources to provide the required care."

2005—An anonymous tip leads to revelations of "significant problems with the quality of care" for surgical patients at the VA's Salisbury, North Carolina, hospital, according to congressional testimony. One veteran who sought treatment for a toenail injury died of heart failure after doctors failed to take account of his enlarged heart, according to testimony.

2006—Sensitive records containing the names, Social Security numbers, and birthdates of 26.5 million veterans are stolen from the home of a VA employee who did not have authority to take the materials. VA officials think the incident was a random burglary and not a targeted theft.

2007—Outrage erupts after documents released to CNN show some senior VA officials received bonuses of up to $33,000 despite a backlog of hundreds of thousands of benefits cases and an internal review that found numerous problems, some of them critical, at VA facilities across the nation.

2009—The VA discloses that than ten thousand veterans who underwent colonoscopies in Tennessee, Georgia, and Florida were exposed to potential viral infections due to poorly disinfected equipment. Thirty-seven tested positive for two forms of hepatitis and six tested positive for HIV. VA Director Eric Shinseki initiates disciplinary actions and requires hospital directors to provide written verification of compliance with VA operating procedures. The head of the Miami VA hospital is removed as a result.

2011—Nine Ohio veterans test positive for hepatitis after routine dental work at a VA clinic in Dayton, Ohio. A dentist at the VA medical center there acknowledged not washing his hands or even changing gloves between patients for eighteen years.

2011—An outbreak of Legionnaires' disease begins at the VA hospital in Oakland, Pennsylvania, according to the *Pittsburgh Tribune-Review*. At least five veterans die of the disease over the next two years. In 2013, the newspaper discloses VA records showed evidence of widespread contamination of the facility dating back to 2007.

2013—The former director of Veteran Affairs facilities in Ohio, William Montague, is indicted on charges he took bribes and kickbacks to steer VA contracts to a company that does business with the agency nationwide.

2014—CNN reports that at least nineteen veterans died at VA hospitals in 2010 and 2011 because of delays in diagnosis and treatment. Three months later, at least forty veterans died while waiting for appointments to see a doctor at the Phoenix Veterans Affairs Health Care system, CNN reports. The patients were on a secret list designed to hide lengthy delays from VA officials in Washington, according to a recently retired VA doctor and several high-level sources.

While this list seems rather lengthy, it could have run much longer as well. It illustrates that the Vietnam veteran's reluctance to even use this system is more than justified. Instead, the veterans are forced to use whatever remedies they can find in the private sector or just leave their problems untreated.

Approximately 30 percent of men and 27 percent of women have had PTSD at some point in their life following Vietnam. These findings, obtained approximately a decade after the end of the Vietnam War, found that for many veterans, their PTSD had become a chronic (that is, persistent and long-lasting) condition. As of 2015, psychological surveys suggest that some two hundred and seventy-one thousand veterans of the war may still have full post-traumatic stress disorder. And for many vets, the PTSD symptoms are only getting worse with time.

The VA now states that it is committed to provide the most effective, evidence-based care for PTSD. It has created programs to ensure VA clinicians receive training in state-of-the-art treatments for PTSD. The VA trains clinicians to use Cognitive Processing Therapy (CPT) or Prolonged Exposure (PE), which are proven to be effective treatments for PTSD.

The National Center for PTSD was created in 1989 within the Department of Veterans Affairs in response to a congressional mandate (PL 98-528) to address the needs of veterans and other trauma survivors with PTSD. The center was developed with the ultimate purpose to improve the well-being, status, and understanding of veterans in American society.

Although the direction of this book is toward the Vietnam War veteran, it would be naïve to think that PTSD is not a risk for all the servicemen and women who have witnessed combat and other stress-related military experiences since then. Soldiers who served in the Persian Gulf War in Operation Desert Storm, Operation Enduring Freedom, Operation Freedom's

Sentinel, Operation Iraqi Freedom, Operation New Dawn, Operation Inherent Resolve, and all other named or unnamed conflicts that have put them in harm's way must be made aware of the invisible wounds they may carry now or that may surface later in their lives. It is our prayer that all may seek help and find a better course of treatment than previous warriors. May God bless them.

EPILOGUE

Admitting to the world that I am not bulletproof, even though I was fortunate enough to survive Vietnam, was quite difficult. On the contrary, I am quite vulnerable and can finally admit that I was wounded by the war. It took fifty years and some great VA doctors to get me to admit that I have carried PTSD all these many years.

I am still undergoing treatment in the VA hospital and may for the rest of my life. I am seeing a wonderful doctor monthly and also attending group therapy sessions with some of my fellow veterans on a weekly basis.

What I have learned is that I am not alone and there are so many other vets who continue to suffer every day. Many of them have fought and continue to fight even bigger demons, drugs, alcohol, homelessness, failed relationships, and many other challenges as a direct result of the war.

The effects of drug and alcohol abuse have been rampant as many vets struggle to cope. Most have lived in denial of their problems for many years. Many failed attempts at getting "clean" when they were repeatedly confronted with their own problems. Usually, they were forced into some type of rehabilitation due to minor crimes they had committed to support their habits as their lives slowly deteriorated.

Friends and family strove to support them early on in their struggles and tried to get them into treatment but, after many relapses, even friends and family had finally given up on them.

They could no longer be reliable enough to hold down a job and spiraled to lower and lower jobs as their habit took more and more control of their lives. Soon the jobs ran out and they were unable to support themselves by any legitimate means; homelessness would soon follow for most.

I was one of the lucky ones to have a great family support network, a wonderful wife who stayed by my side through the good and the bad, even though I never shared anything about the war with any of them until this past year. Fortunately, I was never a drug user during my service or in civilian life.

I was blessed to have caring parents who grounded me, my brothers, and sisters in faith and gave us a moral compass that would serve us well in facing life's challenges.

Family, children, and work kept me very busy for all those years, keeping my mind occupied and, for the most part, preventing me from dwelling on thoughts of the war.

I can't tell you how this story ends because it is still ongoing. I am much more optimistic now than I was a year ago that I am in a better place than I was in the past. Thank you, my family, dear friends, great doctors, and fellow vets, for helping me to get to this place. More to follow...God willing.

Veteran at the Wall
Image credit: Owen Franken/Corbis via
Getty Images

Tom Pisapia

ACKNOWLEDGMENTS

I would like to thank my brother Paul and my good friend Tom Pisapia for their help and support in the writing of this memoir. They were there when, for the first time ever, I spoke of Vietnam. Like my brother Paul, looking at me in surprise on that very first day, said, "You never told me anything about this!"

What followed were meetings with the three of us in Paul's garage twice a week and, of course, a few beers were consumed as well.

I talked in bits and pieces about Vietnam in the random order that they came back to me. Sometimes repeating the same story and sometimes expanding on one, as more and more memories, some fuzzy and some too vividly clear, returned.

Tom wrote down many of these ramblings, and asked questions. As the dialogue became more fluid, we communicated by email in between meetings on a myriad of topics and events.

Those twice weekly meetings lasted over a year and always ended with a group hug, and most of the time we were all in tears.

Hopefully, we were able to present these thoughts in a more cohesive order than they surfaced in my consciousness.

I need to give a huge thank-you to my sister-in-law, Karen, for putting up with the three of us in her garage for all this time. Without her patience, none of this would have been possible. Love you, Karen!

I also wanted to post a picture here of Paul, Tom, and me but my brother refused to allow it. So, I found an old photo of Paul from his high school days. He is the one on the left...

Tom Pisapia

REFERENCES

Chapter 1

Anxiety and Depression Association of America, ADAA, Symptoms of posttraumatic stress disorder (PTSD), https://adaa.org/understanding-anxiety/posttraumatic-stress-disorder-ptsd/symptoms

US Department of Veterans Affairs, PTSD: National Center for PTSD, https://www.ptsd.va.gov/index.asp

Mayo Clinic, Post-traumatic stress disorder (PTSD), https://www.mayoclinic.org/diseases-conditions/post-traumatic-stress-disorder/diagnosis-treatment/drc-2035597

Chapter 2

Image Credit: Jeep with Searchlight, Dean Cherry, http://www.ndqsa.com/vnphotosh.html

Chapter 4

The Sun Also Rises, Ernest Hemingway, Charles Scribner's Sons, New York, 1926

Chapter 5

Tactical-Life, May 8, 2018, photo by US Marine Corps/Cpl. Natalie A. Dillon

Image Credit: Door Gunner, U.S. Marine Corp/ Cpl. Natalie A. Dillon

Chapter 6

armedsavagesix3.blogspot.com/2012/12/ fire-support-base-buttons

War Stories of an Armed Savage-Part 3, FSB Buttons

FSB Buttons early 1970, aerial photo by Ken Filmore

War is Boring, Vietnam Was the Last Hurrah for the Army's Giant Searchlights, October 7, 2015, http://armedsavagesix3.blog-spot.com/2012/12/fire-support-base-but-tons.html

Image Credit: Jeep with Searchlight, Dean Cherry, http://www.ndqsa.com/vnphotosh. htmlImage Credit: Deuce with Quad 50s, Army Transportation Museum

Chapter 7

Grant Singleton, International Rice Research Institute, Pili Drive, Los Baños, Laguna 4031, Philippines, By Leon Watson, https://www.dailymail.co.uk, published December 4, 2013; updated December 5, 2013

Vietnamsoldier.com, "A Year of my Life, Burning Shit: A How to Dispose of Waste Instructional," by Chris Woelk, April 12th, 2017, with photo credit to Randy Barnes, https://vietnamsoldier.com/burning-shit-a-how-to-dispose-of-waste-instructional/

Food Vendor, Image Credit: HOANG DINH NAM/AFP via Getty Images

Image Credit: Burning shit, Randy Barnes Image Credit: Shit Patch, Chris Woelk

Chapter 9

History.com editors, "The Tet Offensive," October 29, 2009, updated June 6, 2019, https://www.history.com/topics/vietnam-war/tet-offensive

Wikipedia.org, "The Massacre at Hue," also *Time Magazine*, "The Massacre at Hue," October 31, 1969, https://en.wikipedia.org/wiki/Tet_Offensive#cite_note-Dougan-Weiss8-16

We Are the Mighty.com, "Warriors in their Own Words: A day in the life of a Vietnam War combat medic," Tim Kirkpatrick Feb. 21, 2018, https://www.wearethemighty.com/history/warriors-in-their-own-words-a-day-in-the-life-of-a-vietnam-war-combat-medic?rebelltitem=5#rebelltitem5

"Their brothers' keepers: Medics & corpsmen in Vietnam," by Jerome Greer Chandler, VFW Magazine, January 11, 2018

Image Credit: Medics, Horst Faas

Chapter 10

Wikipedia.org, "Indigenous peoples of the Central Highlands in Vietnam", https://en.wikipedia.org/wiki/Montagnard_(Vietnam)

Kokomo perspective.com., "Tribes aided American soldiers in the Vietnam War," by Joyce Alpay, Aug 11, 2014, http://kokomoperspective.com/kp/tribes-aided-american-soldiers-in-the-vietnam-war/article_90f-f267a-1d9e-11e4-b2bb-0019bb2963f4.html

Image Credit: George Esper: The Eyewitness History of the Vietnam War 1961-1975, Associated Press, New York 1983

Chapter 11

US Department of Veterans Affairs, "Facts About Herbicides and Public Health, Agent Orange", https://www.publichealth.va.gov/exposures/agentorange/basics.asp

Jets Spraying Herbicides in Cambodia, Image Credit: Bettmann / Getty Images

Chapter 12

100% Alert and Then Some!, Copyright 2002 Ray Sarlin, with permission granted to copy and print. Reprinted from the 1st Bn (Mech) 50th Infantry website http://www. ichiban1.org/. rws@173rdAirborne.com.

Chapter 13

Military Factory, by Dan Alex, last edited 9/26/2016, https://www.militaryfactory. com/smallarms/detail.asp?smallarms_ id=295

The Grunt, The On-line Vietnam Resource Site, Tactics used in Vietnam, https://www. grunt.com/?gclid=Cj0KCQjwuJz3BRDTARI-sAMg-HxUaEQ9t2vFiQGySA34D9PgHdW-0C8xg_uvXWjeJCOvuiYEDnZwYI84saAp-GjEALw_wcB

Retrieved by Memoweb from http://www.soft. net.uk/entrinet/tactics7b.htm at 02/12/01

US Army, Counterinsurgency Lessons Learned #60, 10th September 1966, https://history.army.mil/html/books/us_army_coun-terinsurgency/CMH_70-98-1_US%20 Army_Counterinsurgency_WQ.pdf

WeAretheMighty.com by Blake Stilwell, June 18, 2019, https://www.wearethemighty. com/history/unexploded-ordnance-vietnam

Image Credit: U.S. M2 60mm Mortar, Curio-sandrelics via Wikipedia

Image Credit: Mortar Shells, BidLink

Image Credit: VC Mortar Crew, Library of Congress

Image Credit: VC Soldiers, Source Unknown

Image Credit: 106mm M40 Recoilless Rifle, ForgottenWeapons.com, https://www.for-gottenweapons.com/106mm-m40-recoil-less-rifle-history-and-firing/

Chapter 14

Wikipedia.org, "Hooch maid"

Air Mobility Command Museum, Airlift During the Vietnam War

Wikipedia.org, "Lockheed C-130 Hercules"

Image Credit: AC-130A Plane, United States Air Force

Chapter 15

http://www.militarypolicevietnam.com/OtherThings.html, "Other Things," Copyright (c) 2001-2002 INFANTRYMEN.NET, The Roanoke Times, "More veterans commit suicide than were killed in Vietnam," November 10, 2017, John Ketwig, author of "...and a hard rain fell: A G.I.'s True Story of the Vietnam War", Macmillan 1985

Stars and Stripes, "VA reveals its veteran suicide statistic included active-duty troops," Nikki Wentling, June 20, 2018

Wikipedia.org, "United States military veteran suicide", https://en.wikipedia.org/wiki/United_States_military_veteran_suicide

Chapter 16

army.gov.au/our-history/primary-materials/

vietnam-1962-to-1972/battle-of-coral-bal-moral, "Battle of Coral-Balmoral"

Wikipedia.org, "Beehive anti-personnel round", https://en.wikipedia.org/wiki/Bee-hive_anti-personnel_round

Chapter 17

Wikipedia.org, "M42 Duster", https://en.wiki-pedia.org/wiki/M42_Duster

Image Credit: How Flecchettes Work, The Guardian

Image Credit: Flecchette Shell, Source Unknown

Chapter 18

Wikipedia.org, "Chindits", https://en.wikipe-dia.org/wiki/Chindits

Wikipedia.org, "Meal, Ready-to-Eat", https://en.wikipedia.org/wiki/Meal,_Ready-to-Eat

Meyer, A.I. and Klicka, M.V., "Operational Rations, Current and Future of the Depart-ment of Defense," Technical Report Natick TR-82/031 (September 1982)

Image Credit: C Rations, Mesa Historical Museum

Image Credit: MCI Rations, United States Air Force

Chapter 19

History.com editors, "Vietnam War Protests," Feb 22, 2010, published by A&E Television Networks, https://www.history.com/topics/vietnam-war/vietnam-war-protests

Wikipedia.org, "1968 Democratic National Convention", https://en.wikipedia.org/wiki/1968_Democratic_National_Convention_protest_activity

Stars and Stripes, "Chicago Democratic convention in 1968 embodies clash over future of America," October 1968, Dianna Cahn, cahn.dianna@stripes.com

Chapter 20

The Armies of the Night, Norman Mailer, New American Library, 1968, "History of

PTSD." (Dec 26, 2019). Traumadissocia-tion.com. Retrieved Dec 26, 2019 from http://traumadissociation.com/ptsd/history-of-post-traumatic-stress-disorder.html

The American Psychiatric Association (APA), DSM–5: Frequently Asked Questions, https://www.psychiatry.org/psychiatrists/practice/dsm

CNN politics, "The VA's troubled history," Michael Pearson, CNN, updated May 30, 2014

Smithsonian Magazine, "Over a Quarter-Million Vietnam War Veterans Still Have PTSD," Brian Handwerk, SMITHSONIANMAG.COM, July 22, 2015

US Department of Veterans Affairs, "PTSD: National Center for PTSD, History of PTSD in Veterans: Civil War to DSM-5," Matthew J. Friedman, MD, PhD, Senior Advisor and former Executive Director, National Center for PTSD, https://www.ptsd.va.gov/professional/treat/essentials/history_ptsd.asp

Congressional Research Service, "US Periods of War and Dates of Recent Conflicts," updated August 27, 2019

Chapter 21

Times Square, Image Credit: Lt. Victor Jorgensen/US Navy/The LIFE Picture Collection via Getty Image

Moratorium to End the War image, Image Credit: Charles H. Phillips/The LIFE Picture Collection via Getty Images

Epilogue

Veteran at the Wall, Image Credit: Owen Franken/Corbis via Getty Images

Still Alive: My journey through war, combat and the struggles of PTSD. And the Perils of Addiction. (And stage four cancer), Rusty Lee, AuthorHouse, 12/1/2011

Although I did not use any material from the above book, I did read it during my research. It had a dramatic influence on my insight into the subject. Its powerful and well-written firsthand account gave me an indelible appreciation for the role of hope and faith in all our lives.

TP